To Karla Beelen,

SYSTEMS THAT SHAPE(D) BLACK AMERICA

I wrote this book because I truly love studying Black History + wanted to share key learnings, I wasn't taught in school. I hope you enjoy this book, learn a few new things + share learnings with others. I truly appreciate your support ☺ Thank you !!!

Tracee N. Bruce
7/2/22

SYSTEMS THAT SHAPE(D) BLACK AMERICA

40 Mini Lessons Outlining Defining Moments from Slavery to Modern Day

By

TRACEE N. BRUCE

THEE TNB ENTERPRISES, LLC

Muskegon Heights, MI

2022

SYSTEMS THAT SHAPE(D) BLACK AMERICA:
40 Mini Lessons Outlining Defining Moments
from Slavery to Modern Day
by Tracee N. Bruce

Copyright © 2022 Tracee N. Bruce

Because of the vast nature of the internet,
any web addresses or articles contained in this book may
have changed since publication and may no longer be valid.

For information or permission requests, please contact
Thee TNB Enterprises, LLC at www.TheeTNB.com

ISBN: 979-8-9855591-0-1 (Paperback)
ISBN: 979-8-9855591-1-8 (EPUB)
ISBN: 979-8-9855591-2-5 (PDF)
SBN: 979-8-9855591-3-2 (MOBI)

Library of Congress Control Number: 2022900247

Front cover image © by Alex Bland – Black Liberty

Printed in the United States of America

DEDICATION

"Bringing the gifts that my ancestors gave,
I am the dream and the hope of the slave. I rise. I rise. I rise."
– Dr. Maya Angelou

This book is dedicated to my ancestors who probably
couldn't imagine the life I'm living today…

This book is also dedicated to my parents, the two people
I see myself turning into every day. I am so thankful for the
unconditional love and support you showed me every day of my life.
I am blessed beyond measure!

To my daddy, James Bruce
Thank you for loving me, instilling pride in me, teaching me family
history, Black history, American history, politics, entrepreneurship, and
how to be a critical thinker. This book is a natural extension of you and
the lessons you taught me, Tamara, Shica, and so many others throughout
your life. Sleep in heavenly peace…I love and miss you so much!!!

To my momma, Mary Ray Bruce
My ballroom dancing diva, you are the epitome of wisdom, kindness,
and selflessness. You're beautiful on the outside but so much more on the
inside. Thank you for teaching and showing me love, compassion, and
the importance of "letting things go." There is not one important event in
my life that you weren't present; you never missed a band concert, school
event, choir program, etc., and I appreciate it. You sacrificed daily for
me, Tamara, and Shica, and made it look easy. Without your practical life
lessons, common sense, and teachings on how to "rig things up," I'm not
sure where I'd be! I love you so much!

Thank you!!!

*"Those who do not learn history
are doomed to repeat it."*
– George Santayana

CONTENTS

FOREWORD

P art of understanding any "thing" is to trace it back to its origins. Origins are important because they can reveal intent and motivation. In this book, *Systems that Shape(d) Black America: 40 Mini Lessons Outlining Defining Moments from Slavery to Modern Day,* the origins of race and how it was created to subjugate Black people is discussed. The 400 years covered in this book highlight the reality of a nation that has always used race to determine an individual's worth and value (or lack thereof). We must see that there is nothing color-blind or neutral about race. Race was created in America to dominate Black people. The creation of race laid the foundation for both Chattel Slavery and Jim Crow, two events in which we are still feeling their impact. Today, when we look at our criminal justice system and our racially segregated neighborhoods, we see how race continues to lay the foundation for the differential treatment of Black Americans. I believe that America has had and will always have a race problem until these truths are acknowledged and appreciated. America cannot undo what it chooses not to fully understand.

Education has always been a tool for Black people to combat society's social ills (e.g., racism and prejudice) and advance our position in American life. In this book, *Systems that Shape(d) Black America: 40 Mini Lessons Outlining Defining Moments from Slavery to Modern Day,* Tracee Bruce teaches us not only about the cruel and unjust realities that Black people have endured over the years, but she also sheds light on events where Black people came together, fought back, and ultimately affected change. We must never lose sight of how important it is to fight! Fighting is a survival technique we as Black people cannot afford to lose.

Systems that Shape(d) Black America: 40 Mini Lessons Outlining Defining Moments from Slavery to Modern Day is a love letter to Tracee's father, her family, and her community. Through the use of "mini lessons," she meticulously recounts historical events from the past and reminds us how these events have shaped and continue to shape not only Black America, but America at large. Despite the social progress we as Black people have made in this country over centuries, racism and inequality persist. On many social indicators (e.g., education, income, health, etc.), Black Americans are still disadvantaged compared to White Americans. On average, Black children are suspended or kicked out of school at higher rates than White children, Black employees are paid less than their White counterparts for the same position, and the life expectancy for Black Americans is less than that of White Americans.

I have known Tracee for over 30 years. We grew up together and have remained close friends as adults. We've seen each other celebrate life's "highs" and mourn life's "lows." She has always been passionate about community and giving back. It was important for her to share a history that was never taught in school. She spent years researching the information that is in this book all while maintaining a full-time job! No one paid her or promised her anything if she wrote this book. It simply was something that she wanted to do and so she did it. That's the Tracee I know…strong-willed and true to her convictions. I am so proud of the work she has produced here. I am impressed with the amount of information she includes. For me, it took graduate school and thousands of dollars in student loan debt to learn about many of the topics she covers in this book. I am honored to play a (small) role in this project.

I have always been fascinated with people's understanding of race and how that understanding impacts society. I have dedicated the past ten years of my life to studying race and racism at the University of Illinois at Chicago (UIC). During this time I have obtained three master's degrees: a Masters of Education in Youth Development, a Masters of Arts in Sociology, and a Masters of Education in Measurement, Evaluation, and Statistical Analysis. I have written two master's theses. My first thesis, *Self-Efficacy's Impact on African American Youth's Academic Performance: A Gendered Experience,* compares the relationship between self-efficacy and academic achievement for Black boys and Black girls. My second thesis, *The Nature of Contemporary Prejudice*, examines the structure of White

Americans' racial attitudes. It is my second thesis that led me to pursue a doctoral degree in Sociology, which I plan to complete later this year (2022). My dissertation, *Black Racial Attitudes in Chicago*, explores the structure of Black Chicagoans' racial attitudes and examines the relationship between these attitudes and their social class.

I have published a number of articles and have presented at numerous conferences on topics ranging from Black mothers' perception of the role of race in her child's education, my first published article back in 2017, to my most recent article published last year exploring the intersection of Black and White American's racial and gender attitudes. In addition, my work on who supports workplace diversity policies has been featured in *Harvard Business Review* and *Work in Progress: Sociology on the Economy, Work and Inequality*. Throughout the majority of my graduate studies, I worked in the Office of Diversity where I helped develop and administer sensitivity and bias training programs for the UIC campus community.

This book is a labor of love from Tracee to us! She has given us a great gift with *Systems that Shape(d) Black America: 40 Mini Lessons Outlining Defining Moments from Slavery to Modern Day*. As a race scholar, I believe that the "mini lessons" Tracee shares in this book are fundamental to understanding how race works in America. I recommend that you not only read this book, but that you also engage with its content through personal reflection and meaningful conversations with others. We must make sure that this book "lives" and not become just another item that takes up space on our bookshelves or coffee tables. There is a popular saying that those who fail to learn from history are doomed to repeat it. The limited attention and narrow focus Black people are given in American history narratives is repugnant. Many of us have grown up with an incomplete or distorted account of American history. If you truly believe that Black history is American history, then we must do our part to share our history with the hope that future generations will learn what it truly means to be Black in America.

– Danny L. Lambouths III, M.Ed., M.A.

INTRODUCTION

R acial equity has been a passion of mine for as long as I can remember. It was a passion of my father and often discussed in our household while growing up. From the time I was a young girl, I remember family discussions centered on the root causes of inequities and how to overcome them. I now recognize many of these discussions as survival methods and success strategies unique to the Black community.

I fondly remember my dad, sitting me and my sisters down for one of his "talks." These talks often lasted hours, extending late into the night. We sleepily listened while he told us stories passed down to him—oral accounts that had traveled through his family for generations. I have no doubt that this part of him came directly from his ancestors, the Griots of Western Africa. My dad never went to Africa, but there are things in DNA that transcend space, time, and circumstances.

He told us stories that his grandparents and other family members shared with him, things that happened during Chattel Slavery, and other important events. He often discussed his experiences as a boy growing up in the segregated South and as a preacher's kid.

Two stories that are particularly relevant to my family currently are about Blanche K. Bruce and Bruce's Beach. Blanche K. Bruce was one of the first Black senators in the United States in the 1870s. My family is currently researching to determine if he is one of our ancestors. Bruce's Beach is located in Manhattan Beach, California, and was once a prominent Black beachfront resort owned by our relatives whose land was taken in the 1920s by the city. For many years, there has been an ongoing effort to pass legislation that will return the land back to the descendants of the Bruce family and hopefully provide restitution for the loss of revenue of nearly a hundred years. Finally, on September 30, 2021, California Governor Gavin Newsom signed SB 796 legislation that will enable the beachfront property to be returned to its rightful owners. Property seizure is not unique to our family, it happened to many Black families in this country. Hopefully, the return of Bruce's Beach will set a precedence for this nation to return other stolen property back to their Black owners.

My dad also taught us many lessons about Black history, American history, politics, and more. He instilled pride in us, telling us that we would change the world, own companies, and work for ourselves, affirming our gifts and talents. He even talked about our future offices, how they would be decorated with pictures of our grandmothers. He was such a proud and brilliant man. His stories and lessons were detailed, frequently recalling dates and times with uncanny accuracy. I now wonder if he had a photographic memory. Often these stories would go on for hours until my mom would yell, "James, let those girls go to bed!" to our relief.

At the time, I would grow weary of listening, but it was in those years of hearing all of those stories and history lessons that my love for genealogy, Black history, American history, politics, and entrepreneurship was birthed. I later discovered that most of these interests and passions tend to be hereditary, a family trait. As I meet new family members, many of whom my dad never met, the interests and passions are unmistakably similar.

Currently I am researching my maternal family history. I know a lot about my grandparents and their upbringing in the segregated South, but I also want to learn more about their ancestors. My maternal grandfather Sim Ray, is a local community leader who was awarded the key to the city in our hometown as well as had the honor of a community center being named after him in 2022. I often wonder where his characteristics come from and look forward to learning more about his lineage. Family history is too important not to know and pass along. I encourage others to learn their family history as well.

As a school-aged girl, I particularly loved Black History Month and learning about the Civil Rights Movement. My parents had a collection of Ebony Pictorial History of Black America volumes that I would study. I was fixated on Dr. Martin Luther King, Jr., Coretta Scott King, and many others. At my church, I always participated in the annual Black history programs coordinated by Deacon James Rowan, a community leader in my hometown. Although I always felt my passion for Black history and racial equity was a little strange to have growing up, I could not shake it. As I grew older, I took some courses about Africa and African American studies in college, but never knew how to turn this passion into a career in the business world. At that time, I was not interested in becoming a teacher. However, I never stopped researching and learning, reading books, watching documentaries, and studying on my own.

Fast forward to 2018, I was introduced to equity work while briefly employed at a nonprofit organization whose mission is to eradicate racial disparities and inequities in early childhood. It was there that I was introduced to the targeted universalism and structural fairness models and attended Health Equity & Social Justice workshops. Doing this work, I was finally able to make a connection on how to use my passion for racial equity in a business setting.

In 2020, the killing of George Floyd and the presidential election led to another defining moment in my life. Given the current heightened racial climate in the United States, my desire to expand my work and knowledge on racial equity issues increased exponentially. I was very disturbed by the political and racist arguments that I saw on the news and social media, and I wanted to do something about it. I decided to create a series of flashcards for all communities, but particularly the Black community, on the intentional systems that have shaped the current reality for Black people in America.

As I worked on the flashcards, I embarked on an amazing opportunity. My current employer selected me as one of their fellows to participate in a two-year racial equity fellowship. The goal of this fellowship is to develop public policies and corporate engagement strategies that will address systemic racism by creating race equity solutions. I began to learn much more information that I wanted to share, and my flashcards turned into this book.

When I take time to reflect, I realize the biggest reason I wrote this book is for the young girls, like my younger self, who love Black history and politics and often wonder and ask important questions such as: How did Black people stop being enslaved? Why are Black citizens still being treated differently? Why are neighborhoods still segregated? I want them to know that their curiosity is not strange, but amazing! There are systemic facts that I believe young girls and everyone else should know.

This book takes you on a 40-day journey from Chattel Slavery to the Modern Day era, with mini lessons highlighting some of the insurmountable odds Black people have faced in this country, while celebrating their shocking survival. Each of the 40 mini lessons represents one decade of enslaved Africans and their descendants being in America. This book intends to spark interest, educate, and inspire discussions about past systems that are currently shaping reality for Black people in America. Many of today's current political strategies are repeats of past tactics already used in America's history. We must educate all communities on how we got to this point and how the consequences of voter suppression and other actions created today's society. There is no way to fully capture over 400 years of Black history in only 40 lessons, but this book provides a comprehensive overview.

My intention is to educate as many people as possible. I did the research, and this is my attempt to walk others through history from the Black perspective and to identify how key decisions are still impacting us today. I also want this book to serve as a broad history lesson, as I'm disturbed by many of the fragmented and misleading "arguments" and "facts" I see debated on television, social media, and other outlets. I understand the Black community is not a monolith, many of the conclusions in this book represent my research and perspective, including my lived experiences and that of those in my network.

There are clear links to past policies that have shaped the current realities for Black people. As a Black woman, there is no escaping this reality; it impacts my family, friends, and myself. Instead of complaining about these injustices, I chose to work to bring about solutions and change. I am compelled to do this work in honor of my ancestors and descendants. It is past time to educate ourselves and our children.

I recommend reading one or two mini lessons a day, as there is a lot of information to absorb. This book is suitable for middle school aged readers and older. I hope that parents read these mini lessons with their children, teachers with their students, and book clubs read it together. I also hope these mini lessons spark interest in particular topics and that readers will be inspired to research further and learn more. Please note this book is about enslaved Africans and their descendants, and I refer to them by different names based on the language of the mini lessons' respective time period (e.g., Africans, Enslaved, Black, etc.). Also, I purposely used the term "enslaved" instead of "slaves" to show my respect and dignity for their lives. The system of slavery was something that happened to them and not who they were as people. They were much more than slaves...

This book is also my love story to Black Americans, those who were enslaved from Africa and their descendants. They endured unimaginable horrors (many were intentionally planned) throughout America's history for generations. Yet they survived and their descendants are still present in America today, continuing the fight for equality. Their unlikely survival is something we should be aware of and also celebrate, an extreme source of pride. Black Americans are truly magical people with superhuman, magical blood running through our veins!

To my beloved nephews and nieces:
Todd, Jonathan, Jordyn, Skylar, and Braylen
Here is my attempt to pass down Paw Paw's tradition to you…
☺

PART 1

CHATTEL SLAVERY ERA
(1619–1865)

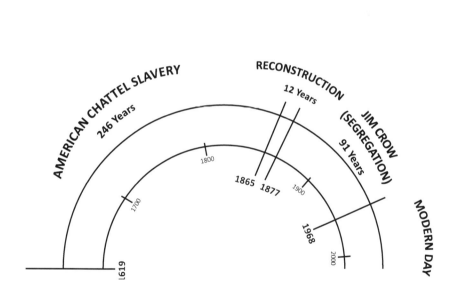

TRANSATLANTIC SLAVE TRADE/ MIDDLE PASSAGE (1500s–1870s)

The *Transatlantic Slave Trade* is responsible for the forced migration of captured African men, women, and children by European slave traders, mainly to the Americas. This slave trade system is estimated to have occurred from the 1500s to the 1870s (more than 370 years). Known as the "Triangular Trade," this voyage involved three routes: Europe to Africa (to transport goods such as knives, guns, cloth, tools, and brass dishes), Africa to the Americas, known as the *Middle Passage* (to transport captured Africans for forced labor), and from the Americas back to Europe (to transport materials produced on slave plantations such as sugar, rice, tobacco, rum, and cotton).

Completely dehumanized and treated like savage beasts, the captured Africans were chained together on cargo ships with little room to move, sometimes less than eighteen inches apart for weeks to months. They were deprived of all human comfort and often unable to communicate with each other, as they spoke many different languages. Bodily functions and atrocities occurred in these tight spaces including sleeping, weeping, eating, urination, defecation, menstruation, vomiting, sexual abuse, rape, birth (at times to their captors' babies), and death. The inhumane conditions incurred on the slave ships led to many diseases, such as influenza, measles, scurvy, smallpox, and dysentery. To add insult to injury, captured Africans were often forced to entertain the crew by dancing and singing.

Captured Africans did not meekly accept their fate; approximately one out of ten slave ships experienced resistance, ranging from individual defiance (e.g., committing suicide by refusing to eat or jumping overboard) to full-blown mutiny (e.g., fighting to overthrow the ship). Suicide attempts were so common, that many captains placed netting around their ships to prevent loss of human cargo in order to protect their profit margin. Sharks regularly followed slave ships due to the number of dead bodies or dying Africans that were thrown into the ocean.

The total number of Africans captured is not known. It is estimated that between twelve to fifteen million Africans, primarily from Central and West Africa, made the 21-to-90-day terror-filled voyage amid vile conditions and despicable, overcrowded ships. Many scholars agree that nearly as many Africans died crossing the Middle Passage as those who reached the end of the voyage. This does not account for the millions of Africans estimated to have died fighting against their would-be captors, who never made it on board the slave ships.

The Transatlantic Slave Trade was outlawed in 1808 in the United States (however domestic slave trading within the United States remained until Chattel Slavery was abolished in 1865) but continued in other parts of the Americas until the 1870s. This slave trade system was a part of the larger European Slave Trade, which is estimated to have occurred from the 1440s to the 1870s. Over the course of roughly 430 years, it is estimated that twenty to thirty million Africans were captured and transported.

Today, there are tens of millions of people of African origin who, because of the Transatlantic Slave Trade, live in the United States, the Caribbean, Brazil, other countries in the Western Hemisphere, and elsewhere outside of Africa.

RELIGION

Religion has played a huge part in creating racial inequalities in America, beginning with Chattel Slavery. Much of early American Christian identity was based on proslavery theology including the naming of slave ships and the sponsoring of journeys often by churches. Some catholic churches in the South relied on plantations and slave labor to help finance the livelihoods of priests and nuns and to support their religious projects and schools. At various moments in American history, the church was the largest corporate slaveholder in Florida, Louisiana, Maryland, Kentucky, and Missouri.

The church justified Chattel Slavery by rationalizing they were Christianizing and civilizing their African captives. Some theologians believed it was "divine order" that brought Africans to America enslaved. Their enslavement would allow them to receive the Christian message, thus resulting in their eternal souls being "saved" from hell. However, enslaved Africans already had diverse religious practices when they were brought to America. Many practiced African spiritual traditions, about twenty to thirty percent were Muslim, and some had already learned of Christianity. Since most Americans were not familiar with African religious practices, they did not respect nor value them.

Slaveholders were often encouraged by preachers to allow enslaved people to attend worship services, in their attempt to indoctrinate them. Worship services were often held in separate gatherings led by White proslavery ministers, who regularly preached sermons encouraging the enslaved to obey their earthly masters. These "men of God" argued that the sermons would promote docility. Using Christian values to justify Chattel Slavery and unequal treatment of the enslaved and their descendants, can also be found in the Lost Cause ideology. This ideology uses Christian values as one of many justifications that Southern Confederate states used for fighting the Civil War in order to keep the institution of Chattel Slavery. However, as Black people learned to read English, many immediately began to read the Bible and protest the idea of a biblical justification for slavery.

During the Jim Crow period, "Christian Identity" and the Ku Klux Klan (KKK) were often viewed as synonymous and played a huge role in terrorizing Black people. Many members of this terrorist group were White churchgoers, who were powerful businessmen and politicians also serving as deacons, Sunday school teachers, and financial supporters in the church. Prior to the Civil Rights Act of 1964, it was normal to see members of the KKK dressed in their robes while attending worship services. The KKK rode around in white hoods with a Bible in hand. The "burning of the cross" has been consistently used as a symbol of intimidation by the KKK, but also as a symbol of Christian fellowship. Cross burning ceremonies during KKK meetings included Christian prayer, worship songs, and other overtly religious symbolism. KKK members believed they were honoring God with their actions.

The Black church has played a pivotal role in the African American experience. In 1758 (over 100 years before Chattel Slavery legally ended), the first recorded Black congregation was organized near Mecklenburg, VA on the plantation of William Byrd. Prior to emancipation, religious exercises conducted by enslaved participants were closely monitored by White Americans to detect plans for escape or insurrection. After emancipation, Black churches throughout the nation offered African Americans refuge from oppression and focused on the spiritual, secular, and political concerns of the Black community, which is referred to as "social gospel." Many White conservative evangelicals today often oppose "social gospel" and see advocating for Black Lives Matter or immigrant rights as political activities rather than moral obligations.

In the Modern Day era, the Black church is still the cornerstone of the African American community and the role of religion in shaping racist ideologies still exists. According to a survey conducted by the Public Religion Research Institute (PRRI) in 2018, racism among White

Christians is higher than non-religious White Americans. White Christians are about thirty percent more likely to say monuments to Confederate soldiers are symbols of Southern pride rather than symbols of racism. White Christians are also about twenty percent more likely to disagree with the following statement: "Generations of slavery and discrimination have created conditions that make it difficult for Blacks to work their way out of the lower class."

Many Black Americans in the Modern Day era believe that racism among White Christians, as referenced in the PRRI survey, was apparent by the way some White evangelicals spewed racist hate and birther conspiracy theories against America's first Black president, Barack Obama.

1619

In August of *1619*, the first group of twenty to thirty captured Africans arrived in Virginia. Upon arrival, this group was documented and has been historically referred to as "20 and odd Negroes." This group included men, women, and children kidnapped from their villages in the Kingdom of Ndongo in modern Angola. They were a part of a larger group heading to Veracruz, Mexico, and were taken by English pirates after an attack on the Portuguese slave ship that was transporting them.

Even before the encounter with the pirates, this journey was traumatic filled with terror, hunger, and death for the roughly 350 Africans on board the *San Juan Bautista*. Of the roughly 350 Africans on the slave ship, roughly 143 died during the Middle Passage, about sixty were taken by English pirates on two separate ships (White Lion and Treasurer), and roughly 147 people were eventually taken to Veracruz. When the "20 and odd" enslaved Africans arrived in Virginia on the White Lion, Governor George Yeardley and his head of trade, cape merchant (treasurer) Abraham Piersey, bought them in exchange for food. It is reported that the Treasurer also arrived in Virginia, a few days after the White Lion and dropped off roughly three people, before taking the estimated twenty-seven remaining enslaved Africans to Bermuda.

Although it has been documented that the first free and enslaved Africans arrived in what would become the United States in the 1500s, it is noteworthy that this transaction in 1619 is credited as a turning point for slavery. This transaction in 1619 is considered to be the start of America's uniquely brutal race-based Chattel Slavery system. Prior to 1619, some historians believe that enslaved Africans were treated more like indentured servants. Indentured servants were usually treated as humans and not commodities, with a fixed amount of time for servitude.

This system of Chattel Slavery created centuries of unique, lifelong, brutal treatment of enslaved Black people that has become part of the American fabric of society. It is well documented that descendants of enslaved Africans in America continue to face unequal treatment over 400 years after this initial transaction in 1619.

CHATTEL SLAVERY (1619–1865)

American *Chattel Slavery* was the uniquely brutal, legal institution of enslaving Africans and their descendants solely based on race and was very different from most forms of slavery that preceded it. During American Chattel Slavery, enslaved Africans were treated as property, with little to no legal rights, able to be bought, sold, and forced to work without wages. Prior to the European Slave Trade, most people became enslaved as a result of war, with losers becoming manpower for labor. By contrast, Europeans created an economic enterprise by capturing, shipping, and selling other human beings based on race.

Slavery is a brutal institution in any society, but especially so with the treatment by Europeans during Chattel Slavery. Enslaved people, including pregnant women and children, were brutally punished for any perceived defiance. Common punishments included whippings, body mutilations, children sold, rape, forced reproduction, being burned alive, and death. There was little to no recourse to justice for enslaved people; slaveholders rarely, if ever, received backlash or punishment for harsh treatment or killing those they enslaved.

In many societies, although slavery was practiced, it was more akin to indentured servitude. Indentured servants were usually treated as humans, during Chattel Slavery enslaved Africans were treated as property. Indentured servants were typically allowed to be educated, America is the only known country with anti-literacy laws that prohibited their enslaved population from learning to read or write. Indentured servants had a fixed amount of time for servitude and then were freed. During Chattel slavery it was rare for enslaved people to be freed. Indentured servants' children were usually born free, in America generations of people of African descent were born and died enslaved. This natural increase allowed the colonies to become a slave nation.

In an effort to shift blame for the treatment of Africans during Chattel Slavery, there is a common argument by slave apologists that Africans are the ones who sold other Africans to White colonists and helped create the institution of Chattel Slavery in America. Although it is well known that Africans sold other Africans into slavery, they treated their conquered as indentured servants, not chattel, and had no way of knowing the conditions that enslaved Africans faced in America. There is no way of knowing how African nations would have responded if they were aware of the inhumane treatment and hardships enslaved Africans and their descendants endured in America, since they did not behave that way towards those they conquered.

When captured Africans were physically removed from their homelands during Chattel Slavery, they were stripped from their languages, spiritual practices, craftsmanship, skills, music, dance, art, and other important elements of their culture. However, a small number managed to pass these traditions down to their offspring.

American Chattel Slavery was abolished in 1865 with the passing of the Thirteenth Amendment. This brutal institution lasted at least 246 years, but most likely longer as enslaved Africans were documented in the 1500s. However, 1619 is credited as a turning point for slavery with the start of America's brutal race-based Chattel Slavery system.

This system of selling other humans laid the foundation for the world's wealthiest nation, the United States of America. For centuries, the lives and free labor of enslaved Africans by Europeans were used to cultivate crops such as cotton and sugar cane. Products and profits from this system successfully turned the United States into a leader in global trade and a world power that is still present in the Modern Day era. Slaveholders, much like today's top one percent of wealthy Americans, were extremely influential in local and national politics. Slaveholders used their wealth and influence to create many of America's current institutions, largely benefitting their descendants and other White people who also benefitted from America's racist rules and customs (e.g. legal segregation).

In the Modern Day era, many powerful Americans and profitable large corporations have links to America's slave past and most likely benefit from generational wealth. Enslaved Africans had no wealth, land, or influence for their descendants to inherit.

RACE FACTORED INTO LAW (1600s)

During American Chattel Slavery, racial and class hierarchies were *factored into law,* with racial distinctions being prioritized. Those who committed the same crimes were being punished drastically different based on race. Black people in America were being enslaved for life while protections for White people were being formed. The earliest documented case was in the 1640s when John Punch, a Black indentured servant, escaped servitude with two White indentured servants. Upon being captured, the White indentured servants only received additional years of servitude, while Punch was sentenced to enslavement for the rest of his life.

During Bacon's Rebellion (1675–1676), free and enslaved Black people aligned themselves with poor, free, and indentured White servants against the government. Historians believe this rebellion accelerated racial distinctions associated with punishment and slavery. The people in power were alarmed when these groups united and they created more stringent laws that defined status based on race and class. Those in power also convinced poor White people they were superior to Black people as a way to control and prevent future rebellions.

These laws and actions were the beginning of a more rigid system of racial slavery accompanied by improved status for White servants. Racial distinctions were prioritized over class to prevent another Bacon's Rebellion. For example, some White free workers and indentured servants were given authority and power over enslaved Black people by receiving opportunities such as becoming "overseers." Also, White free workers and indentured servants, unlike free and enslaved Black people, could not be stripped naked and whipped. As historian Edmund S. Morgan suggested, "a hardening of racial lines contributed to a growth in a commitment to democracy, liberty, and equality among White men."

In the modern American criminal justice system, treatment is often based on race and class, effectively resulting in two systems. Oftentimes, Black people suffer disproportionately in the criminal justice system because of their skin color and low financial resources, which is evident in the current era of mass incarceration. Events such as Bacon's Rebellion helped lay the foundation for today's criminal justice system.

SLAVE CODES (1691)

Slave codes were laws governing the newly created Chattel Slavery system in the Americas. Slave codes were vague, with much of the actual practice of slavery being a matter of traditions rather than formal law. However, most rules included in the slave codes were more concerned with the rights and conduct of free Black people instead of governing enslaved Black people.

During Chattel Slavery, Black people became free in numerous ways including as a result of the Revolutionary War, immigration from places such as Saint-Dominique, and through manumissions (formal acts of emancipation by slaveholders). Black people were granted manumissions in numerous ways including obtaining "favor" from slaveholders often as a result of being their offspring, being "dumped" by their enslavers as they aged and were no longer considered "useful," and "willed" free upon their slaveholder's death.

In 1691, South Carolina was first to enact slave codes adopted from Jamaica and served as the model for many other colonies in the United States. Colonies and states passed laws that discriminated against free Black people, with the purpose of preserving slavery. Due to their potential influence on enslaved people, free Black people presented a challenge to the boundaries of a White-dominated society. Slave codes denied free Black people basic human and citizenship rights, such as the right to freedom of assembly (including for worship), vote, bear arms, education, free speech, and the right to testify against White people in court.

After the Civil War, in an effort to control newly freed Black people, Southern states enacted Black codes. These laws resembled slave codes and most notably restricted the movement of formerly enslaved people.

Lawmakers knew that newly freed Black people had meager resources and generally lacked adequate food, clothing, and shelter. Newly freed Black people were landless and uprooted, in desperate need of work. By restricting the movement of formerly enslaved people, Black codes constrained many of them to work as plantation laborers, often for their former enslavers at abysmally low wages.

SLAVE PATROLS (1704)

Slave patrols were organized groups of armed White men who monitored and enforced discipline upon the enslaved population in America's Southern states. Beginning in South Carolina in 1704, slave patrols spread throughout the colonies. Their primary function was to police the conduct of enslaved people, especially those who escaped or were viewed as defiant. Other functions included monitoring enslaved people's movements, suppressing rebellions, and protecting White people's property. Slave patrols also formed river patrols to prevent escape by boat. During these times, enslaved people were often mistreated by slave patrols despite having permission to travel.

As the population of enslaved Black people increased, especially with the invention of the cotton gin and the cultivation of sugar cane, so did White people's fear of resistance and uprisings. Their biggest concern was enslaved people holding their enslavers and other White people against their will on plantations, since that is where enslaved populations were largest. Incentives, such as money and tobacco, were initially offered to White people urging them to be more vigilant in capturing runaway enslaved people. Slave patrols were formally created when this approach failed.

Laws were put into place to control the actions of both Black and White people. White people were legally obligated to monitor Black people's actions. Black people (free and enslaved) were subjected to questioning, searches, and other forms of harassment. Enslaved people who were encountered without traveling passes from their White enslavers were returned to their slaveholders, as stated in the slave codes. Expected punishment for runaway enslaved people included whippings and beatings.

However, most enslaved people feared the threat of being sold and ultimately separated from their families more than physical punishment.

After the Civil War, slave patrols developed into Southern police departments and carried over tactics such as systematic surveillance, curfew enforcement, etc. It is widely believed that the origins of slave patrols still influence modern-day police department tactics such as stop-and-frisk, which often operate under the assumption of guilt or suspicion when interacting with the Black community.

ANTI-LITERACY LAWS IN THE UNITED STATES (1740–1865)

For over a hundred years, it was against the law for White people to teach free or enslaved Black people how to read or write in any form. *Anti-literacy laws* in many slave states before and during the Civil War were a natural extension of the slave code system. The slave code system primarily focused on the conduct of free Black people, whereas anti-literacy laws included enslaved Black people as well.

Alabama, Georgia, Louisiana, Mississippi, North Carolina, South Carolina, and Virginia all passed anti-literacy laws between 1740 and 1834, which were important to many White people for numerous reasons. These laws reinforced the belief that African people were inferior to White people. Some White people feared that Black literacy would prove a threat to Chattel Slavery which relied on the dependence of enslaved people on their slaveholders. Many White Southerners were illiterate, so it was vitally important to prevent Black people from learning to read and write in order to maintain the myth of White supremacy. Some anti-literacy laws arose from concerns that literate enslaved people could forge documents required to escape, which many did attain freedom in this manner. Anti-literacy laws also arose from fears of uprisings and rebellions, especially during the time of Nat Turner's slave rebellion in 1831.

Learning to read gave enslaved people access to abolitionist literature, which flooded the South with news that openly encouraged enslaved people to rebel and advocated against slavery. Black people who disobeyed anti-literacy laws were severely punished, sentenced to whippings, amputations, and other disciplinary actions. White people who disobeyed these laws received less severe consequences such as fines, jail time, and occasional physical punishments.

Restrictions on the education of Black people were not limited to the South. While teaching Black people in the North was not illegal, many Northern states banned Black students from attending public schools.

Despite efforts by plantation owners to stop Black people from learning how to read and write, many strategies emerged within the Black community to undermine their attempts. Enslaved people who became literate did so in various ways: some taught themselves, some learned to read from other literate enslaved people, and others were taught by their slaveholder's children. Some slaveholders had literate enslaved workers undertake business transactions and keep accounts, seeing this as an economic benefit. Other slaveholders believed that enslaved people should be able to read the Bible.

Many of these anti-literacy laws became obsolete in 1865 when Chattel Slavery was abolished and the Freedmen's Bureau was created. The Freedmen's Bureau assisted with clothing, food, shelter, banking services, and education for newly freed Black people. However, the Freedmen's Bureau was met with much resistance by many White Southerners and failed to make real strides towards racial equality. Ultimately Congress conceded to the pressure from White Southerners and dismantled the Freedmen's Bureau in 1872.

To date, the United States is the only country known to have anti-literacy laws for its enslaved population. Many researchers today believe we are still taking education away from Black children in the same spirit of these anti-literacy laws. This is evidenced by Black kids being disproportionately suspended from school for minor infractions such as being in the hallway at the wrong time, having a hoodie over their head, or wearing the "wrong" hairstyle. Law enforcement is asked to patrol and enforce minor nonviolent violations, handcuffing Black children in their schools and leading them to jails and courtrooms full of other Black children—helping to facilitate the modern school-to-prison pipeline.

THREE-FIFTHS COMPROMISE (1787)

E nslaved people were not viewed as full human beings. The issue of enslaved representation was argued during the 1787 United States Constitutional Convention. At this time, free Black people were counted as full citizens for representation. Southern states were motivated to keep and protect slavery. Delegates debated whether and how enslaved people would be counted when determining a state's total population. This number determined how much a state would pay in taxes, the number of seats in the House of Representatives, and the number of electoral votes for presidential elections. *The Three-Fifths Compromise* was reached among state delegates.

The Compromise counted three-fifths of each state's slave population (three out of every five enslaved people). This gave Southern states more seats in the House of Representatives and more electoral votes than if enslaved people had been ignored, yet fewer seats than if enslaved and free people had been counted equally. Since enslaved people could not vote, leaders in slave states would have the added benefit of increased representation in the House of Representatives and the Electoral College. The Three-Fifths Compromise also increased the federal tax burden of slaveholding states. This was the law for almost one hundred years.

Finally, in 1868, Section 2 of the Fourteenth Amendment repealed the Three-Fifths Compromise. It stated that "representatives shall be apportioned...counting the whole number of persons in each State, excluding Indians not taxed." In theory, this law granted citizenship to all Black people including those who were formally enslaved in the United States. Citizenship included the right to vote for all males (women were not legally able to vote at this time). However, individual states still denied Black men the right to vote. It was not until the Fifteenth Amendment was ratified in 1870 that all Black men were granted the right to vote nationwide.

Former slave states created a variety of strategies to disenfranchise Black voters after the Reconstruction era came to an end in 1877, while also obtaining the benefit of increased representation based on the total population. These measures were effective in giving White Southerners even greater voting power than they previously had in the Chattel Slavery era. It inflated the number of Southern Democrats in the House of Representatives and the number of votes they could exercise in the Electoral College for presidential elections. It counted the total number of Black Americans in the state's population but denied them the right to vote.

The strategies used to disenfranchise Black voters after Reconstruction were the first of many attempts to suppress Black votes, which can still be seen today, more than 140 years later. Consider polling tax as an example. In the late 1800s, Florida created the poll tax system requiring its citizens to pay cash in order to vote. Appearing to be race-neutral, poll taxes disproportionately affected African Americans since many had extremely low incomes and could not afford to pay and thus could not vote. This law was so successful that within twenty years, all former Confederate states had adopted poll taxes.

Currently, in the Modern Day era, Florida Republican officials are accused of repeating this tactic by requiring citizens with a prior felony conviction to pay all applicable court fines, fees, or restitution before their voting rights will be reinstated. This policy disproportionately targets African Americans. According to the United States Census Bureau, Black Americans were roughly seventeen percent of Florida's population in 2019, yet account for almost forty-eight percent of the prison and jail population per the Sentencing Project. A 2019 Kaiser Family Foundation (KFF) report finds that Black Floridians have a poverty rate of 19.8 percent, more than double that of White Floridians at 9.2 percent, which makes both the repayment of debt and the opportunity to vote more difficult.

FUGITIVE SLAVE ACTS (1793 & 1850)

The *Fugitive Slave Acts* were a pair of federal laws in the United States that governed the capture and return of runaway enslaved people. The Fugitive Slave Act of 1850 required all citizens to aid in the capture of fugitive enslaved Black people. Lack of compliance was considered breaking the law. The previous 1793 Act enabled slaveholders to pursue runaway enslaved people, but it was difficult to enforce. The 1850 Act created a legal obligation, regardless of moral views on Chattel Slavery, to support and enforce the institution.

Black people had no defense nor right of participation in the enforcement of the 1850 Act; if a White person incorrectly challenged the status of a free Black person, the Black person could not defend him or herself and could be enslaved. As a result of the passage of the Fugitive Slave Acts, some free Black people were wrongfully captured and sold into slavery. This caused a huge threat to free Black people. In fact, in 1860, the year of Abraham Lincoln's election and the beginning of the Southern states' withdrawal from the United States to form the Confederate States of America, there were a total of 488,070 free Black people living in the United States. Free Black people represented about ten percent of the entire Black population, and the majority (fifty-four percent) of them lived in Southern slaveholding states.

During Chattel Slavery, Black people became free in numerous ways including as a result of the Revolutionary War, immigration from places such as Saint-Dominique, and through manumissions (formal acts of emancipation by slaveholders). Black people were granted manumissions by obtaining "favor" from slaveholders often as a result of being their offspring, being "dumped" by their enslavers as they aged and were no longer considered "useful," and "willed" free upon their slaveholder's death.

The Fugitive Slave Act of 1850 divided the nation and helped to create the path to the Civil War. It was virtually unenforceable in certain Northern states due to widespread opposition. During the 1850s, the Underground Railroad reached its peak, and many enslaved people fled to Canada to escape. By 1860, only around 330 enslaved people had been returned to their Southern slaveholders.

Congressmen who opposed the Fugitive Slave Acts introduced bills regularly to repeal them, but the laws persisted into the Civil War. It was not until 1864 that both Fugitive Slave Acts were repealed by Congress, 71 years after the first Act was passed.

One of the effects of the Fugitive Slave Acts in the Modern Day era is the widely-held belief that the testimony of White people is given more weight than that of Black people in the criminal justice system.

SLAVERY'S DEADLY COMMODITIES (EARLY 1800s)

By the late 1700s, Chattel Slavery in the United States was on the decline as tobacco, once a major crop, had worn out the soil in many areas. It was during the early 1800s when the cultivation of *cotton* and *sugar cane* increased the dependence on enslaved labor in the South. Growing cotton and sugar cane were labor-intensive activities, and that labor was supplied primarily by enslaved people.

The cotton gin was patented by Eli Whitney in 1794, making cotton a global economic force. Whitney's cotton gin (short for engine) led to cotton being cleaned (separating cotton fibers from their seeds) faster. The result was an exponential increase in the production and selling of cotton.

Around 1795, a Frenchman in New Orleans named Jean Etienne Bore discovered a method of boiling off sugar cane until it turned into crystals, thus creating granulated sugar. Demand for sugar skyrocketed and the cultivation of sugar spread throughout the Southeast. However, sugar cane was a brutal crop requiring constant attention and a six-day work week. The cultivation of sugar cane often disfigured, burned, and killed enslaved laborers. The life span could be as little as seven years for an enslaved person on a sugar plantation. Unfazed, plantation owners literally worked their enslaved laborers to death. To prepare for this high "turnover," they constantly brought new enslaved individuals to replace the dying. The British poet William Cowper wrote, "I pity them greatly, but I must be mum/ For how could we do without sugar or rum?" Making money by selling sugar to sweeten food and drinks took precedence over human life and set the tone for Chattel Slavery in America.

Enslaved people faced increasingly brutal conditions, as the products of their labor secured the nation's position as a global economic and political powerhouse. In 1808, the United States abolished the Transatlantic Slave Trade, creating a slave shortage. This increased the domestic slave trade within the United States. Enslaved people were sold from state to state as the market dictated, often breaking up families. An estimated one million enslaved people were sent to the Deep South to work the fields. Another way that slaveholders increased their slave labor was through births, essentially turning enslaved women into baby factories.

The cultivation of cotton and sugar cane increased the value of enslaved workers. In 1800, the average cost of an enslaved person was around $50; by 1850, it was more than $1,000. In 1800, the number of enslaved people in America was roughly 900,000; by 1860, on the eve of the Civil War, the number was estimated at four million. Slaveholders had created a lucrative, free labor force system where they could keep, sell, rape, or kill as they saw fit. To defend the system, slaveholders often used the Bible as a rationale stating that slavery was good for enslaved workers and a normal human condition.

MEDICAL EXPERIMENTS
ON BLACK PEOPLE

R acism has been prevalent in *medical experiments* and research at the cost of Black lives, leading to mistrust in the Black community of the medical field. The following are just a few examples of medical experiments and research that violated the rights of Black people.

Dr. James Marion Sims, the founder of modern gynecology, was a physician in the mid-1800s. He was credited with the creation of the first vaginal speculum and pioneered a surgical technique to repair vesicovaginal fistula (a painful abnormal hole between the bladder and uterus that happened as a result of childbirth). Sims began his career in a makeshift hospital that he built in his backyard. There he conducted surgical experiments on countless enslaved women without anesthesia or their consent, usually in front of other doctors. Ignoring their screams, Sims argued their race made them more durable, and thus well suited for painful medical experimentation. The racist belief that Black people have a higher pain tolerance is still prevalent today; a basic web search will reveal many studies that provide evidence of racial bias in pain treatment including a study conducted at the University of Virginia and published on April 4, 2016, in the Proceedings of the National Academy of Sciences.

The Tuskegee Syphilis Experiments, conducted between 1932 and 1972, is another example of Black people being used as medical test subjects. Hundreds of Black men were given the syphilis disease without their knowledge or consent. Participants of the study were told they were receiving free health care from the federal government, but the actual purpose was to observe untreated syphilis. The participants were never treated with penicillin, and what was intended to be a six-month study was extended to forty years. Long-term effects of their untreated syphilis included issues with mental functions, balance, memory loss, vision loss, and some deaths.

The "Mississippi Appendectomies" (1920s–1980s) refer to the unnecessary and involuntary sterilization (removing a person's ability to reproduce) of poor, Black women considered unfit to have children. During this time, states such as North Carolina and Mississippi operated eugenics and sterilization programs. North Carolina sterilized almost 8,000 people over the span of forty-five years, forty percent of whom were women of color. Until the 1960s, most hospitals in the United States were segregated by race, but integration threatened to break down the Jim Crow system. It was a common belief among Black people in the South that Black women were routinely sterilized without their informed consent for no valid medical reason, but as a backlash to integration, as a form of population control, and as a result of negative stereotypes about Black people.

Henrietta Lacks (1920–1951) was a young wife and mother, who was diagnosed and treated for cervical cancer. During her treatment, her biopsied cancer cells were used for medical research without her knowledge or consent at Johns Hopkins Hospital in Baltimore, Maryland. Her cancer cells are the source of the HeLa cell line, the first immortalized human cell line, meaning the cells rapidly reproduce in a laboratory setting. The HeLa cell line is one of the most important cell lines in medical research. The widespread illegal use of her cancer cells has led to many medical break-throughs in vaccines, cancer treatments, in vitro fertilization, etc. Scientists have grown as much as fifty million metric tons of her cells since the 1950s, and there are almost 11,000 patents involving HeLa cells. The cells of Henrietta Lacks proved invaluable for medical research. Healthcare labs and companies have gained financially from using HeLa cells for decades, with no compensation for Henrietta or her family.

In the Modern Day era, a growing body of research shows that centuries of racism (both interpersonal and structural) in the United States has had a profound and negative impact on Black people and other communities of color. Many organizations, medical associations, hospital systems, state and municipal governments as well as federal government agencies such as the Centers for Disease Control and Prevention (CDC) publicly acknowledge that racism negatively affects the mental and physical health of millions of people. Many of these entities recognize racism as a public health threat, emergency, and/or crisis and is actively working on strategic actions to combat racism and its negative effects on Black people and other communities of color.

JUSTIFY RACISM THROUGH MENTAL ILLNESS

Mental illness has been used as an attempt to justify racism, throughout the history of the United States. In 1851, Southern physician Samuel Cartwright believed he found a rational explanation for enslaved people who wanted to escape their slaveholder—a mental illness called *drapetomania*, a Greek word roughly translating to "runaway slave" and "crazy." He reassured slaveholders that it was entirely curable by "whipping the devil" out of enslaved people or cutting off both of their big toes, sometimes both "treatments" were used.

Cartwright also claimed the existence of another "mental disorder" that he called *dysaesthesia aethiopica*, which supposedly made Black people lazy in their work. According to him, *dysaesthesia aethiopica* affected more free Black people than enslaved Black people, because free Black people did not have enslavers to care for them.

These types of racist beliefs endured through the 1960s when psychiatrists diagnosed "angry" politically active Black men involved in the Civil Rights Movement with "protest" psychosis instead of condemning the violent injustices they were protesting.

However, in the Modern Day era, there is a legitimate mental illness being linked to the traumatic effects of Chattel Slavery. In 2005, psychologist and professor Dr. Joy DeGruy released her groundbreaking book, *Post Traumatic Slave Syndrome: America's Legacy of Enduring Injury and Healing.* Post Traumatic Slave Syndrome (PTSS) describes the multigenerational trauma experienced by African Americans that lead to undiagnosed and untreated Post-Traumatic Stress Disorder (PTSD) in enslaved Africans and their descendants. It is an existing condition, a consequence of the multigenerational oppression of Africans and their descendants, which results from centuries of Chattel Slavery. PTSS differs from PTSD; PTSD results from a single trauma experienced directly or indirectly; PTSS, on the other hand, is from people experiencing racism through generations as well as individuals facing continuous stress from daily racism.

More entities and people are now recognizing the effects racism can have on one's psyche, especially in light of racial tensions that are currently present in the United States today. Many organizations, medical associations, hospital systems, state and municipal governments as well as federal government agencies such as the Centers for Disease Control and Prevention (CDC) publicly acknowledge that racism negatively affects the mental and physical health of millions of people. On October 29, 2021, the American Psychological Association (APA) apologized for its long-standing contributions to systemic racism and is developing a long-term plan to counter racism by creating a more equitable, diverse, and inclusive association, discipline, and society going forward.

DRED SCOTT V. SANDFORD (1857)

The *Dred Scott v. Sandford case of 1857* was a landmark decision in which the Supreme Court of the United States agreed with lower courts, ruling the Constitution did not include American citizenship for Black people. Therefore, the rights and privileges of the Constitution could not apply to Black people, regardless of whether they were enslaved or free.

Dred Scott was an enslaved man who sued for his freedom and that of his wife, Harriet Robinson Scott, and their two daughters Eliza and Lizzie, but was unsuccessful. In *Dred Scott v. Sandford*, Scott sued his enslaver, John Sanford, claiming that he and his family should be granted their freedom because they had lived as enslaved people in Fort Snelling, a free territory in Missouri, as well as Illinois and the Wisconsin Territory for years. Chattel Slavery was illegal in all of these places. The laws of these areas stated that slaveholders gave up their rights to ownership of enslaved people who stayed there for extended periods of time. Due to a clerical error, the slaveolder's last name was misspelled in this famous case; it was actually Sanford and not Sandford.

The Scotts' legal battle for freedom lasted eleven years. They sued in the St. Louis Circuit Court in 1846 where the Scotts lost due to a technicality. Upon retrial, the family was granted freedom in 1850. However, their holder appealed the verdict, and the case was sent to the Missouri Supreme Court in 1852. The Missouri Supreme Court reversed the St. Louis Circuit Court's decision, returning the Scott family to slavery. The Scotts then filed a federal lawsuit in the Circuit Court of the United States for the District of Missouri in 1853, which also ruled against them, applying Missouri law to the case. The Scotts appealed this decision to the United States Supreme Court in 1856.

On March 6, 1857, the Supreme Court decision in *Dred Scott v. Sandford* was issued, eleven long years after the initial suit. Seven of the nine justices joined in the majority opinion delivered by Chief Justice Roger Taney which stated: "They had no rights which the White man was bound to respect; and that the Negro might justly and lawfully be reduced to slavery for his benefit." *Dred Scott v. Sandford* held that enslaved people were not citizens of the United States and had no right to sue in federal courts. The Supreme Court decision was intended to settle the issue of slavery, but it only intensified the debate.

The newspaper coverage of the court ruling and the eleven-year legal battle raised slavery awareness in non-slave states. The arguments for freedom in this case, were later used by President Abraham Lincoln and helped build public support for the Emancipation Proclamation (1863). It also set the stage for the three constitutional amendments ratified shortly after the Civil War: The Thirteenth Amendment (abolishing slavery in 1865), the Fourteenth Amendment (granting citizenship and civil rights to all Black Americans in 1868), and the Fifteenth Amendment (granting Black men the right to vote nationwide in 1870).

Dred Scott eventually obtained his freedom, but not through the courts. He and his wife were transferred to the Blow family who freed them in 1857. Sadly, Dred Scott died of tuberculosis in 1858, just one year after attaining freedom.

EMANCIPATION PROCLAMATION (1863)

The *Emancipation Proclamation* was a presidential announcement and executive order issued by President Abraham Lincoln, roughly two years into the Civil War. The Emancipation Proclamation granted freedom to approximately 3.5 million enslaved people in the Southern Confederate states (slaveholding states fighting against the United States) if they did not return to the Union (non-slaveholding states fighting on behalf of the United States) by January 1, 1863. It did not apply to an estimated 500,000 enslaved people in the slaveholding Border states (Missouri, Kentucky, Delaware, and Maryland) loyal to the Union. After the Proclamation in 1863, the new state of West Virginia also became a Border state. Lincoln exempted the Border states from the Proclamation because he did not want to tempt them into joining the Confederacy by freeing their enslaved population. He justified this decision as a wartime measure.

When the Civil War began, Lincoln's intent was to get the Confederate states to rejoin the Union and to find a compromise for the opposing sides on slavery, not to abolish it. He would have kept slavery if it meant the South would rejoin the Union. However, when the rebelling Confederate states refused to return to the Union, the Emancipation Proclamation went into effect, circumstances changed rapidly, and public opinion strongly supported the Union. This changed the purpose of the Civil War into a mission to abolish slavery. The irony of the Border states is that they ended up fighting to end slavery, while being slaveholding states.

The Proclamation changed the legal status of enslaved African Americans in the ten rebel Confederate states (Texas, Louisiana, Mississippi, Alabama, Georgia, South Carolina, Florida, Arkansas, North Carolina, and Virginia) from enslaved to free beginning January 1, 1863. Tennessee was another rebel state but is not listed because Union troops had already gained control at the time of the Proclamation. Many enslaved people in Confederate states were not freed immediately by the Emancipation Proclamation, as Southern slaveholders did not share the news of freedom with them. Enslaved people learned of their freedom as the Union army made its way across the South.

The Emancipation Proclamation became an official part of the United States' military strategy. The acceptance of Black men into the Union Army was announced by the Proclamation, enabling them to fight for their own freedom. An estimated 186,000 Black soldiers joined the Union Army by the time the Civil War ended in 1865, and roughly 38,000 lost their lives. Because the Emancipation Proclamation was only a temporary war measure applying to the Confederacy, it did not permanently end slavery in the Border states. The institution of American Chattel Slavery was finally abolished with the ratification of the Thirteenth Amendment in 1865.

The Emancipation Proclamation is considered one of the greatest documents of human freedom and a very important milestone in the long process of legally ending Chattel Slavery.

CIVIL WAR (1861–1865)

The *Civil War* took place in the United States from 1861 to 1865. It was fought between Northern states loyal to the Union and the Southern states that had seceded to form the Confederate States of America. After decades of simmering tensions between Northern and Southern states, primarily over Chattel slavery, but also because of states' rights and westward expansion, the American Civil War began in 1861.

The Union consisted of the following twenty non-slaveholding states: Maine, New York, New Hampshire, Vermont, Massachusetts, Connecticut, Rhode Island, Pennsylvania, New Jersey, Ohio, Indiana, Illinois, Kansas, Michigan, Wisconsin, Minnesota, Iowa, California, Nevada, and Oregon. Abraham Lincoln was their President.

Maryland, Delaware, West Virginia, Kentucky, and Missouri were called Border states, these slaveholding states were also loyal to the Union. Abraham Lincoln was their President.

The Confederacy consisted of the following eleven slaveholding states: Texas, Arkansas, Louisiana, Tennessee, Mississippi, Alabama, Georgia, Florida, South Carolina, North Carolina, and Virginia. Jefferson Davis was their President.

War broke out in April 1861 just over a month after Abraham Lincoln's inauguration as the President of the United States. As a Republican, Lincoln was anti-slavery but had no intention to abolish it. His election outraged the Southern states; they viewed this as a violation of their constitutional rights and a first step to abolish slavery. The North (Union) wanted slavery to end, while the South (Confederacy) wanted to keep slavery. Numerous historians believe that many in the North were in support of freeing enslaved people, not for moral reasons; they just could not compete with the South's free labor market.

A turning point in the Civil War was in 1863, when Lincoln issued the Emancipation Proclamation. The Proclamation would free an estimated 3.5 million enslaved people in the rebel Confederate states if they did not rejoin the Union. However, it did not apply to an estimated 500,000 enslaved people in the slaveholding Border states. The Confederate states refused to rejoin, and the Civil War's mission evolved into freeing enslaved people. Many formerly enslaved people in the Confederate states joined the Union Army and fought in the war. This additional manpower helped secure the Union's victory. Losing enslaved people not only demoralized White Southerners but also deprived them of their labor force. An estimated 186,000 Black soldiers joined the Union Army by the time the Civil War ended in 1865, and roughly 38,000 lost their lives.

The Civil War ended in Confederate surrender in 1865. This conflict was the deadliest and costliest war ever fought on American soil. It is estimated that between 620,000 and 750,000 soldiers were killed, many more were injured and much of the South was left in ruins. Because the Emancipation Proclamation was only a temporary war measure applying to the Confederacy, it did not permanently end slavery in the Border states. American Chattel Slavery was finally abolished with the ratification of the Thirteenth Amendment in 1865.

Chattel Slavery legally ended but the injustices that Black people faced did not. Rather than being included in society as newly freedmen and offered opportunities for advancement, Black people were instead treated in much the same manner as when they were enslaved.

JUNETEENTH (1865)

June 19, 1865, also known as "*Juneteenth*," marks the day that Union soldiers arrived in Galveston, Texas, and informed the enslaved population of their freedom. Sadly, this occurred two and a half years after the Emancipation Proclamation, which had already freed enslaved people in Texas on January 1, 1863. Slaveholders did not inform enslaved people of their freedom when the Emancipation Proclamation went into effect. Later the same year, on December 6, 1865, the Thirteenth Amendment was ratified which abolished the institution of Chattel Slavery forever in the United States. All enslaved people were legally free by the end of 1865.

The formerly cnslaved population in Galveston celebrated after the announcement, and the following year organized the first annual celebration of "Jubilee Day" on June 19. Since then, celebrations have taken on many forms. Early celebrations were used as political and voting rallies for newly freedmen and usually occurred at the beginning of January. In some cities, Black people were banned from using public parks for these celebrations because of state-sponsored segregation of facilities. In response, some of the newly freedmen pooled their funds to purchase land for the annual celebrations. Jubilee Day was known as Juneteenth, by the 1890s.

Political and economic forces significantly reduced Juneteenth celebrations from 1890 to 1908. Texas and all former Confederate states passed new amendments and constitutions that effectively disenfranchised and excluded Black people from the political process. Author Gladys L. Knight wrote that the decline in celebration was also in part because "upwardly mobile Blacks were ashamed of their slave past and aspired to assimilate into mainstream culture. Younger generations of Black people, after becoming further removed from slavery, were occupied with school and other pursuits. Others who migrated to the Northern United States couldn't take time off or simply dropped the celebration" (Encyclopedia of African American Popular Culture, 2011).

Juneteenth celebrations further declined during the 1950s and 1960s, as the Civil Rights Movement focused the attention of African Americans on desegregation. However, Juneteenth was still popular in Texas and celebrated regionally. It soon saw a revival, as Black people began connecting their current struggles to that of slavery's ending.

Over the years, Juneteenth has been steadily gaining popularity with varying official recognitions. Federal legislation had been introduced in Congress on several occasions to make Juneteenth a national day of observance or a federal holiday. Finally in 2021, Congress passed federal legislation and President Joe Biden signed the Juneteenth National Independence Day Act into law on June 17, 2021. Juneteenth is now a public holiday and will be legally celebrated annually on the 19th of June throughout the United States.

Descendants of enslaved people proudly celebrate this holiday as the end of slavery. Many of them recognize this holiday, arguably just as important to the United States as the Fourth of July (Independence Day).

THIRTEENTH AMENDMENT (1865)

O n December 6, 1865, the *Thirteenth Amendment* was ratified, which legally abolished American Chattel Slavery. It stated, "Neither slavery nor involuntary servitude, except as a punishment for crime whereof the party shall have been duly convicted, shall exist within the United States, or any place subject to their jurisdiction." The Thirteenth Amendment was necessary as the Emancipation Proclamation in 1863 did not end slavery for all; those enslaved in the Border states had not been freed.

The Thirteenth Amendment is important and celebrated because it abolished Chattel Slavery; however, it also has a loophole: "*except as a punishment for crime.*" This clause justifies enslaving human beings if they have been "duly convicted" of a crime. Many believe the Thirteenth Amendment's loophole has been used as a means of controlling the rights of Black people through legal incarceration post-emancipation. Instead of truly abolishing slavery, other methods were created to keep Black people enslaved. Black people went from being perceived as docile slaves to criminals, seemingly overnight. This clause is essential to understanding how the United States criminal justice system developed into the roots of today's mass incarceration.

After the Civil War, Southern states immediately began drafting laws designed to lead to the arrest of Black people who were then put back to work (sometimes in prisons that had once been plantations, like Angola in Louisiana) as enslaved people in every aspect but name. This has contributed to America's long history of economic empowerment off the backs of enslaved people. These new laws sent Black people to prison at higher rates than ever before, resulting in what legal scholar Michelle Alexander referred to as a "prison boom," in her book The New Jim Crow.

According to Alexander's book, the criminal justice system was strategically deployed to force Black people back into a system of extreme suppression and control, a tactic that would continue to prove successful for generations to come.

Immediately following the Civil War, Black codes were created for newly freed Black people, restricting their freedom and making it easier to be arrested. Black people were prosecuted for so-called offenses such as vagrancy, breaking curfew, loitering, having weapons, and not carrying proof of employment. These laws were effective as they ensured Black people returned to chains. Violation of the Black codes created convict leasing, a labor system in the American South that leased prisoners out to work in locations such as mines, railways, and plantations. Prisoners earned no pay for their labor, often faced horrific, dangerous, and sometimes deadly work conditions, while states profited.

In the Modern Day era, prison systems are considered slavery of a different name by many. America's prison system is a multi-billion-dollar industry with incarcerated people doing everything from building military equipment to staffing call centers to making office furniture. States and large private companies rely on prisoners for cost savings. Citizens not incarcerated also profit from this system because prison labor saves tax dollars. In 2017, California's government revealed it used incarcerated "volunteer" firefighters which saved taxpayers up to $100 million dollars a year. Today, there are prison inmates all over the country making products and offering services that are sold for profit by companies who split the revenue with the prison. Inmates are often employed to operate and maintain the prison itself, as well as contracted to work for outside agencies or even private companies. For federal prisons, this is done through UNICOR (trademark for Federal Prison Industries), which is the government corporation that sells quality goods and market-priced services made by inmates.

A disproportionate amount of inmates are Black and they contribute significantly to prison labor representing forty percent of the incarcerated population, despite being roughly thirteen percent of the total United States population. According to a PolitiFact report, in 2013 there were more Black men in prison, jail, on probation, or on parole than the number of Black men enslaved in 1850.

These types of prison structures cause alarm. By allowing prisons to do business directly with the private sector, perverse motivations may occur that can lead to more incentives to increase incarceration. Creating more avenues for Black people to be incarcerated, thus "enslaved."

RECONSTRUCTION ERA
(1865–1877)

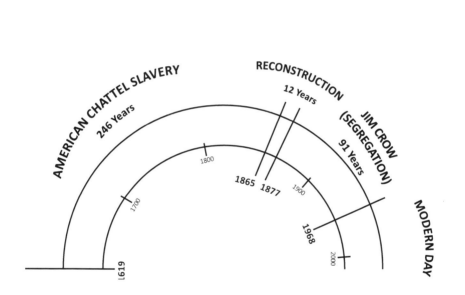

RECONSTRUCTION (1865–1877)

T he *Reconstruction* era was a period in American history that lasted from 1865 to 1877 following the Civil War (1861–1865). It is a monumental chapter in the history of American civil rights. The Reconstruction era was an attempt to rebuild the country and grant civil rights to formerly enslaved and free Black people.

The ratification of three amendments, known as the "Reconstruction Amendments," solidified the constitutional legacy of the Reconstruction era, in particular for newly freedmen. The Thirteenth Amendment, ratified in 1865, formally abolished slavery. The Fourteenth Amendment, ratified in 1868, granted all Black Americans (including newly freedmen) citizenship, thus equal protection under the law regardless of race. The Fifteenth Amendment, ratified in 1870, granted Black men the right to vote nationwide. During this time period, the Republican Party supported civil and voting rights for formerly enslaved people, while the Democratic Party strongly opposed it.

On March 3, 1865, the Freedmen's Bureau Bill became law, sponsored by the Republicans to aid freedmen and impoverished White people in the South. With the help of the Bureau, freedmen began voting, forming political parties, and started managing their own labor in many areas. As a result, the Republican Party elected many African Americans to national, state, and local offices. Black men voting in state and federal elections marked a dramatic social change. At the beginning of 1867, no Black American in the South was elected to political office, but within three or four years into the Reconstruction era, about fifteen percent of Southern legislators were Black—a larger percentage than in 1990. Most of the offices were held at the local level.

This period of Black voters and legislators was short-lived as Southern White backlash took over; widespread violence in the South against freedmen and White people who supported Reconstruction broke out. Most of the violence was carried out by domestic terrorist organizations: the Ku Klux Klan (KKK) being the most popular, the White League, the Red Shirts, and similar organizations who allied with the Southern Democratic Party. They intimidated and attacked Black people seeking to practice their new civil and voting rights. They used intimidation, violent attacks, and even assassination to run Republicans out of office and to suppress the Black vote, leading to Southern Democrats regaining power by the mid-to-late 1870s. In 1871, federal intervention by President Ulysses S. Grant suppressed the KKK. However, Southern Democrats, known as "Redeemers," regained control of the South by controlling state elections, often using fraud and violence. The Reconstruction era officially ended with the Compromise of 1877, formally ending federal protection for newly freedmen.

Despite the Fifteenth Amendment, Black people were not able to vote freely in the South again until the Voting Rights Act of 1965, nearly a hundred years later. A key lesson of Reconstruction and its brutal, racist rollback, according to historian Eric Foner, is that "achievements thought permanent can be overturned and rights can never be taken for granted" (Gates, 2019).

FORTY ACRES AND A MULE (1865)

W hen the Civil War ended in 1865 and the Reconstruction era began, the South was in ruins. The Southern economy was devastated with many of its cities, businesses, and railroads destroyed. Many former slaveholders had fled and their plantations and other property were either destroyed or seized by the federal government. Formerly enslaved people, known as freedmen, found themselves free but without the means to support their families. As a result, the United States federal government had to grapple with complex issues such as unifying the country, the fate of the Confederate leaders, rebuilding the South's economy, and solidifying the legal status of nearly four million newly freedmen.

This difficult period in American history began with ambitious ideas such as General William T. Sherman's Special Field Order No. 15, known as *Forty Acres and a Mule*. On January 12th, 1865, Sherman met with twenty Black ministers who also served as community leaders. They told him that land ownership was the best way for newly freedmen to become economically self-sufficient and enjoy their newfound freedom. Four days after the meeting on January 16th, 1865, Sherman issued the Order temporarily granting newly freed families forty acres of confiscated land on the islands and coastal regions of Georgia, South Carolina, and Florida for Black settlement. Sherman later agreed to loan some of the freedmen army mules (mules were not included in the actual order). Six months after Sherman issued the order, roughly 40,000 newly freedmen lived on 400,000 acres of this coastal land.

In March 1865, Congress seemed receptive to plans for widespread land reform when it authorized the Freedmen's Bureau to divide confiscated land into small plots for sale to Black and loyal Southern White families.

Many believed this policy would be extended to all formerly enslaved people and their families as repayment for Chattel Slavery and their involvement in the Civil War. However, an alternative path was selected and enforced. Although President Abraham Lincoln appeared to support the land reform policy, he was assassinated in April 1865 and his successor, President Andrew Johnson, had other plans. In the summer of 1865, as one of his first acts during the Reconstruction era, President Johnson ordered all land under federal control be returned to the owners from whom it had been seized.

Less than a year after Sherman's Order, the majority of seized land was returned to its former owners, the very same people who declared war on the United States and joined the Confederacy during the Civil War. This included land that most newly freedmen had already settled on. Federal troops evicted tens of thousands of Black landholders, sometimes by force. Some Black people fought back, driving away former owners with guns. In the end, only two thousand Black people retained the land they had been granted and worked on after the Civil War.

The result of these actions was that most newly freed Black people had no resources. They were left with no land or means for financial independence. Plantation owners and other landowners in the South regained their land but needed a labor force to cultivate it. The solution was sharecropping, which matched newly freedmen looking for work with landowners looking for workers. This began the process of rebuilding the nation economically via sharecropping labor contracts that were often unfair and exploitative to newly freedmen. These contracts typically resulted in newly freedmen acquiring large sums of debt. Unable to pay, newly freedmen found themselves trapped on plantations, yet again.

It is difficult to stress how revolutionary the Forty Acres and a Mule order was. It was the first systematic attempt to provide a form of reparations to newly freedmen, by methodically redistributing land formerly owned by Confederates. This Order was considered astonishingly radical for its time. In fact, during this time some claimed this idea was more radical than abolishing the institution of Chattel Slavery, as it would have transformed Southern society. In the Modern Day era, this type of policy would still be considered radical given the current political climate. Imagine how the history of race relations in the United States would be profoundly different if this policy had been implemented, enforced, and expanded. If roughly four million newly freedmen were able to own land and other property. If they had the chance to be self-sufficient economically, to build, accrue, and pass on generational wealth to their offspring. If newly freedmen were able to fully participate in the American dream.

KU KLUX KLAN

The *Ku Klux Klan* (*KKK or Klan*) is an American White supremacist hate group that terrorized African Americans primarily during the Reconstruction era and the Civil Rights Movement.

The Klan was founded in 1865 after the Civil War, and flourished in the Southern United States in the late 1860s and early 1870s, during the Reconstruction era. The organization was created as a backlash to Black men gaining the right to vote and using this power to elect Black legislators and other Southern Republicans into political office for the first time in American history. The Klan initiated widespread violence in the South toward newly freedmen and White people who supported Reconstruction.

The Klan attacked and intimidated Black people seeking to exercise their new civil and voting rights. Klan members used terrorism, intimidation, violent attacks, and lynchings to seriously weaken Black political leadership. As a result of these actions, the Klan successfully ran Southern Republicans out of office, overthrew Republican state legislative gains, and repressed the Black vote. In 1871, President Ulysses S. Grant suppressed the Klan by utilizing the Third Enforcement Act. This Act (sometimes referred to as the Ku Klux Klan Act), was a new law that allowed President Grant the authority to mobilize the United States military anywhere vigilante groups committed violence against African Americans. However, since the Klan had already suppressed much of the Republican vote and removed a significant number of Black and White Republicans from political office, White Democrats, known as "Redeemers," regained control of the South. Redeemers controlled state elections often using fraud and violence, which led to effectively creating Jim Crow laws.

In the 1950s and 1960s, the Klan made a powerful comeback with strong intimidation attacks directed at Black people who wanted to gain equal rights. The Klan opposed the Civil Rights Movement and desegregation. Klan members often used physical violence, bombings, cross burnings, and lynchings to suppress civil rights activists. One of the most heinous crimes the KKK committed during the Civil Rights Movement was the 16th Street Baptist Church bombing that killed four Black girls in 1963.

During this period, the Klan often forged alliances with Southern police departments and governor offices. In fact, many law enforcement officials were Klan members and participated in murders, such as Deputy Sheriff Cecil Price of Neshoba County, Mississippi. Klan members rarely received punishment for their crimes, as Black people were not fully allowed to participate in the criminal justice system in the segregated South. The criminal justice system was primarily comprised of White people including police, prosecutors, judges, juries, and prison officials. However, in the Modern Day era, some of the Klan's cases have been reopened and have resulted in some convictions.

The federal government's relationship with local law enforcement agencies and the Klan, particularly that of the Federal Bureau of Investigation (FBI), was often ambiguous. The first FBI director, J. Edgar Hoover, appeared more concerned with targeting civil rights activists than controlling Klan violence against them. In fact, the FBI began its COINTELPRO program in 1956, which was a series of secret and unlawful projects to infiltrate, disrupt, and destroy civil rights leaders and groups.

There is still some Klan activity in the Modern Day era. The current KKK is not a single organization, but rather one comprised of small independent chapters across the United States. Recent KKK membership campaigns have stimulated anxiety regarding illegal immigration, islamo-phobia, Black political leaders, and same-sex marriage.

LOST CAUSE IDEOLOGY

The *Lost Cause of the Confederacy* (*Lost Cause*) is an ideology that attempts to explain the "true" reasons why Southern states fought in the Civil War, from the Confederate's perspective. In an effort to preserve the honor of the Confederates and the Southern states, the Lost Cause interpretation asserts the South's reasons for fighting the war were fair and heroic. The Lost Cause theory encouraged the belief that American Chattel Slavery was just and moral because it brought economic prosperity. It also promoted the lie that enslaved people were happy, even grateful, for the institution of Chattel Slavery. Most historians view the Lost Cause ideology as a myth.

According to the Lost Cause ideology, the Civil War was a result of overwhelming Northern aggression. The Confederate states had to "fight the war" in order to save the Southern way of life including their Christian values and to protect "states' rights." At the same time, the Lost Cause minimized, if not completely denied, the central role of Chattel Slavery and White supremacy as reasons for the Civil War.

This ideology has evolved and been used to preserve the "Southern way of life" or "heritage" in many waves throughout American history. One wave of Lost Cause activity happened during World War I (1914–1918), as the last surviving Confederate veterans neared the end of their lives. Efforts to preserve their memories increased. In the 1950s and 1960s, another wave of Lost Cause activity occurred in response to growing public support for racial equality during the Civil Rights Movement. During these waves, Lost Cause promoters sought to preserve their movement by ensuring future generations of Southern White Americans learned about the South's "true" reasons for fighting the Civil War. Activities to preserve their movement

SYSTEMS THAT SHAPE(D) BLACK AMERICA

included building Confederate monuments and writing school history textbooks. This ideology helped "justify" White supremacist policies, such as Jim Crow laws.

The Lost Cause ideology has also shaped religious attitudes. For example, surveys conducted by the Public Religion Research Institute (PRRI) in 2018 found that White Christians are about thirty percent more likely to say monuments of Confederate soldiers are symbols of Southern pride rather than symbols of racism. White Christians are also about twenty percent more likely to disagree with this statement: "Generations of slavery and discrimination have created conditions that make it difficult for Blacks to work their way out of the lower class."

Since the end of the Civil War, the personal and official use of Confederate flags has continued under considerable controversy. The Lost Cause beliefs frequently emerge during these types of controversies surrounding the public display of the Confederate flag and various state flags.

Basic assumptions of the Lost Cause ideology have proved long-lasting for many in the modern South. These trends generally persist even in the wake of recent protests for racial justice.

THE COMPROMISE OF 1877

In 1876, the Presidential election results were disputed in three Southern states: Florida, Louisiana, and South Carolina. The winner could not be decided, so there was a deal, or a compromise, between the Democrats and Republicans, known as the *Compromise of 1877*. This informal, unwritten deal ended federal protection for newly freedmen, bringing a formal end to the Reconstruction era and its political and civil rights gains for Black people. This deal is sometimes referred to by Black historians as the "Great Betrayal" because it ended the post-Civil War promises made to Black Americans.

In the Compromise, the Democrats agreed to the Republican candidate Rutherford Hayes becoming president and equal rights for Black people. In return, the Republicans agreed to Democrats controlling the South and the removal of all federal troops from Southern states, who were protecting newly freedmen.

As soon as the troops left, many White Republicans also left, and the Democrats took control. President Hayes kept his campaign promise to the South by restricting federal enforcement of the unpopular Reconstruction era policies: the Thirteenth, Fourteenth, and Fifteenth Amendments. These laws abolished slavery, gave Black Americans the status of citizenship, and granted Black men the right to vote.

The promises of the Democrats to protect the civil and political rights of Black people were not kept. The end of federal intervention in Southern affairs led to extensive disenfranchisement of Black voters. From the late 1870s onward, with Black people unable to vote, Southern legislatures passed a series of racist segregation legislation known as Jim Crow laws. These segregationist laws governed life in the South and suppressed the

Black vote until the Civil Rights Movement of the 1950s and 1960s, almost a hundred years later.

The Compromise of 1877 not only resulted in Black voter disenfranchisement, but also led to racist Jim Crow laws, the sharecropping system, and the spread of the Ku Klux Klan's domestic terrorism dominating the South with lynchings.

PART 3

JIM CROW ERA
(1877–1968)

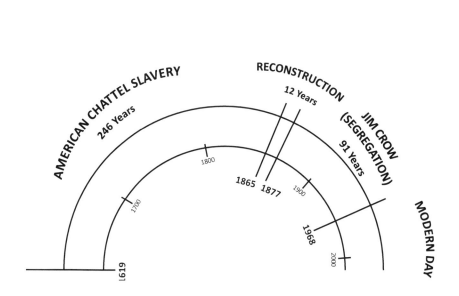

JIM CROW (1877–1968)

A fter the Civil War almost tore the nation apart, Chattel Slavery legally ended but the inequalities that Black Americans faced did not. Rather than being offered opportunities for advancement and inclusion as equal members of society, Black people were treated as little more than enslaved people. Their rights were severely restricted despite being freed. The Compromise of 1877 marked the beginning of *Jim Crow*, effectively ending the Reconstruction era which stopped efforts to provide newly freedmen viable access to economic opportunity and sustained equal rights.

Jim Crow, named after a popular fictional character in a racist minstrel show, was the new system that legalized segregation by race in all aspects of American life for nearly a hundred years. Jim Crow operated primarily, but not exclusively, in Southern and Border states between 1877 and 1968.

During the Reconstruction era, the passage of the Thirteenth, Fourteenth, and Fifteenth Amendments to the Constitution had granted Black Americans the same legal rights and protections as White Americans. As a "backlash" to Reconstruction, Southern states adopted new state constitutions and enacted laws suppressing the civil and voting rights of Black people. In order to keep Black people unequal to White people. With Black voters once again disenfranchised under the guise of "states' rights," racist Jim Crow laws were created, restricting the rights of African Americans.

Under Jim Crow, African Americans were legally relegated to the status of second-class citizens. These laws mandated that Black people be separate from White people on every occasion and segregated all public spaces, including transportation and public schools. It also excluded Black Americans from facilities, juries, jobs, and neighborhoods.

Unfortunately for Black Americans, the Supreme Court helped legitimize Jim Crow laws with the infamous *Plessy v. Ferguson* case in 1896. This decision upheld state-sponsored segregation as constitutional so long as the accommodations were "separate but equal." As long as the facilities provided to each race were "equal," state and local governments could require that services, facilities, public accommodations, housing, medical care, education, employment, and transportation be segregated under this doctrine. In reality, services and facilities for Black people were never "equal" to White people. If the services and facilities for Black people even existed, they were consistently inferior, underfunded, or more inconvenient to access as compared to those offered to White people.

The Jim Crow system also controlled the conduct and etiquette of Black Americans. Black people could not look White people in the eye, could not shake their hands, were not allowed to call them by their first names without a courtesy title, and so on. The Jim Crow laws and system of etiquette were undergirded by violence. Black people who violated Jim Crow norms—for example, drinking from White water fountains or trying to vote—risked their homes, their jobs, and even their lives. White people could physically beat Black people and were rarely punished.

Black people had little legal recourse against these assaults because the Jim Crow criminal justice system was primarily comprised of White people including police, prosecutors, judges, juries, and prison officials. The most extreme forms of Jim Crow violence were lynchings. Lynchings were often public, advertised events where White people, frequently bringing their children, cheered on vicious murders typically carried out by mobs.

The Jim Crow era officially ended in 1968 as a result of the many legal victories gained during the Civil Rights Movement.

SHARECROPPING (1860s–1950s)

Sharecropping often involved unfair and exploitative labor contracts for newly freedmen. It is an example of the United States' failure to provide formerly enslaved people access to economic opportunity, particularly with regard to land ownership. Formerly enslaved people were never given their "Forty Acres and a Mule" as compensation for their unpaid labor at the end of the Civil War in 1865. The Compromise of 1877 exacerbated the economic condition of Black Americans by ending the Reconstruction era and beginning Jim Crow. These events gave Southern states freedom to create an economic system that revived many of the disenfranchising elements of Chattel Slavery.

Plantation and landowners in the South needed a labor force to cultivate their land, and newly freedmen were looking for economic opportunities. The result was sharecropping, which matched newly freedmen looking for work with plantation and landowners looking for workers. With the creation of the sharecropping system, Southern states successfully kept most Black people working on the same land they had worked while enslaved.

Sharecropping was a legal system, in which landowners would rent land to Black farmers (tenants) in exchange for a portion of the harvest. The owners would loan supplies needed to cultivate the land, such as seeds and farming equipment with unfair debt terms to the Black tenant. At the end of each year, charges for the supplies were deducted from the sharecroppers' portion of the harvest, often resulting in a deficit. High-interest rates, weak harvests, and corrupt landowners often kept Black tenants severely in debt, with continual debt being carried over from year to year. Once in debt, the law prohibited sharecroppers from leaving the landowner's property until they were able to repay, thus trapping them on the landowner's property.

The sharecropping system put the majority of newly freedmen back in the position of being enslaved to the landowner, effectively creating slavery under a new name.

Some Black sharecroppers managed to acquire enough money to rent or own their own land, but many more went into debt. They were forced by poverty or the threat of violence to sign unfair and exploitative sharecropping or labor contracts. These contracts left them little hope of improving their situation. Sharecropping, along with tenant farming, had come to dominate agriculture across the cotton-picking South from the late 1860s to the 1950s.

Increasing mechanization of agriculture throughout the 1930s and 1940s eventually brought the institution of sharecropping, which had existed since the Civil War, to an end. This forced many landless Black farmers off the landowners' property. Once again, numerous Black people had no money or land to show for their hard work.

LYNCHINGS/MASSACRES (MOST COMMON 1880s–1960s)

*L*ynchings are another atrocity that became a prominent part of America's history as a result of the Compromise of 1877. The federal government's decision to remove federal troops from the South, ushered in a widespread campaign of racial terror and oppression against newly freed Black Americans.

Lynchings were used as an intimidation tool to keep Black people "in their place." Most of the victims were hanged or shot, but some were burned, castrated, beaten, dismembered (or a combination thereof), usually for an alleged offense, with or without a legal trial. Among the most disturbing realities of lynching was the degree to which some White Americans embraced it. Lynchings were often perceived as joyous moments of wholesome celebration. Lynchings were often advertised events where entire families attended, with mothers and fathers even bringing their young children. More often than not, victims would be dismembered, and mob members would take pieces of their flesh and bone as souvenirs.

The majority of lynchings occurred in Southern and Border states where the resentment against Black people ran deepest, but lynchings also occurred in Northern states. Many White people claimed that although lynchings were distasteful, they were necessary additions to the criminal justice system because Black people were prone to violent crimes. Lynchings were often supported on the popular false belief that they were necessary to protect White women from Black rapists. Under Jim Crow law any interactions considered sexual (whether actual or perceived) between Black males (including boys) and White women were illegal and considered rape.

Most Black people were lynched for advocating for civil rights, violating Jim Crow laws or etiquette, or in the aftermath of race riots. Lynchings usually occurred in small and middle-sized towns where Black people were often economic competitors to local White people, who resented any economic and civil rights gains made by Black people.

Lynchings were usually conducted by mobs and those involved were seldom arrested, and if arrested, rarely convicted. In most cases, the mobs were assisted and helped by law enforcement. Officers would routinely leave a Black inmate's jail cell unguarded after rumors of a lynching began to circulate. This would allow the mob to kill Black suspects before any trial or legal defense could take place.

Lynchings served many purposes and were often considered a uniting point for White communities. These "events" provided cheap entertainment and served as a method of defending White domination. Lynchings helped to stop or slow down social equality movements that threatened White supremacy. Although mobs may lynch several people at a time, they usually directed their hatred towards one victim. The victim was usually a Black man, being used as an example to showcase the consequences of innocent actions such as attempting to vote, applying for a "White man's" job, or simply looking at a White woman. Young Black males including teenage boys were not exempt from lynchings, the horrific murder of fourteen-year-old Emmett Till is a prime example.

Unfortunately for Black people, sometimes the mobs were not satisfied with murdering only a single person or even several victims. Occasionally mobs also infiltrated Black communities, destroying additional lives and property, resulting in race riots and massacres. Their immediate goal was to remove, by death or otherwise, Black people from their community; the ultimate goal was to maintain their White-dominated society.

According to the National Association for the Advancement of Colored People (NAACP), from 1882 to 1968, 4,743 lynchings occurred in the United States. Of the people lynched, 3,446 (72.7%) were Black and 1,297 (27.3%) were non-Black including immigrants. Some of the victims were White and usually lynched for helping Black people, having anti-lynching views, or for domestic crimes. Sociologist Arthur Raper investigated nearly a century of lynchings and concluded that approximately one-third of all victims were falsely accused. These lynching numbers are estimates, as it is known that many lynchings were not recorded.

Black communities faced the constant threat of lynchings and massacres at the hands of White mobs. White mob members did not want to see Black people advance economically, so they destroyed Black communities. Famous examples of massacres include The Red Summer in 1919 and Black Wall Street in 1921.

Many Black people resisted the injustices of Jim Crow, and far too often, paid for their bravery with their lives.

NAACP (1909–PRESENT)

The *National Association for the Advancement of Colored People* (*NAACP*) is America's oldest and largest civil rights organization. It was founded in 1909 by an interracial group consisting of W.E.B. Du Bois, Mary White Ovington, Ida B. Wells-Barnett, and others worried about the challenges facing African Americans, especially after the 1908 Springfield, Illinois Race Riot. The NAACP's initial charter was to champion equal rights, eliminate racial prejudice, and to "advance the interest of colored citizens." Areas of focus included voting rights, legal justice, educational and employment opportunities.

In 1910, the NAACP began publishing a quarterly magazine called *The Crisis*. It became the leading publication for Black writers and was edited by Du Bois for the first twenty-four years. Many of the NAACP's actions focused on national issues; for example, the group launched a massive anti-lynching campaign. This effort increased public awareness of lynchings and is thought to have contributed to an eventual decline in lynchings. Many believe this campaign also helped influence President Woodrow Wilson to denounce lynchings in 1918.

In 1939, the NAACP established the NAACP Legal Defense and Education Fund as an independent legal arm for the Civil Rights Movement. It litigated the landmark case *Brown v. Board of Education* (1954), which outlawed segregation in public schools. Earlier in 1946, the organization had also won a significant victory with *Morgan v. Virginia*, which outlawed segregation in interstate travel, setting the stage for the Freedom Rides of 1961. In 1963, NAACP Field Director Medgar Evers was murdered, propelling the group into national recognition, likely contributing to the passage of the Voting Rights Act in 1965.

In the Modern Day era, the NAACP is still very active in African American advancement; it sponsors campaigns against youth violence, encourages economic enterprise, and leads voter registration drives to increase Black participation in the political process. The group's current mission includes issues such as police misconduct, the status of Black foreign refugees, and economic development. The NAACP also acknowledges and celebrates African American achievement by granting annual awards.

The NAACP is recognized as one of the greatest civil rights organizations in American history.

GREAT MIGRATION (1916–1970)

The *Great Migration* was the relocation of an estimated six million Black Southerners to the urban Northeast, Midwest, and West that occurred around 1916 to 1970. The primary factors for the migration were segregation, discrimination, widespread lynchings, and poor economic conditions in the South, where Jim Crow laws were upheld.

Many Black Southerners headed north to take advantage of the labor shortage in industrial cities during World War I (1914–1918). With wartime production demand increasing, recruiters enticed African Americans to come north, much to the dismay of White Southerners. Black newspapers, such as the *Chicago Defender*, published advertisements for job opportunities available in Northern cities, along with first-person accounts and testimonies. By the end of 1919, an estimated one million Black people had left the South and found jobs in factories, slaughterhouses, and foundries where working conditions were grueling and sometimes dangerous.

While segregation was not legalized in the North (as it was in the South), racism and prejudice were nonetheless widespread. Black people were often confined to overcrowded and run-down housing and were largely restricted to low-paying, menial jobs. There were violent, anti-Black riots, like those during the Red Summer in 1919, as a result of tensions between new Black settlers and recent European immigrants. These groups often competed for jobs and scarce housing. Conditions were not the best for African Americans; however, Northern cities offered economic and educational opportunities far greater than what was available in the rural South.

During the Great Migration, African Americans began to build a new place for themselves in public life. They actively confronted racial prejudice as well as economic, political, and social challenges. African Americans created a new Black urban culture, most notably during the Harlem Renaissance that would exert enormous influence in the decades to come. The Civil Rights Movement also directly benefited from this activism.

Black migration slowed considerably in the 1930s when the country sank into the Great Depression, but picked up again as demand for wartime production increased during World War II (1939–1945). Around 1970, the Great Migration ended, but its demographic impact was profound: In 1900, nine out of every ten Black Americans lived in Southern states, with three out of every four living on farms; by 1970, the South was home to less than half of the country's Black population, with only twenty percent living in rural areas.

THE GREEN BOOK (1936–1967)

The *Negro Motorist Green Book* (*Green Book*) became an invaluable resource for Black people living in and traveling through the United States. It listed business establishments (including Black-owned businesses) across the country that would serve Black customers. Guiding travelers to safe establishments that served a wide range of functions for Black people.

First published in 1936, the Green Book was developed by a Harlem-based mail carrier, Victor Hugo Green. Like most African Americans in the mid-20th century, Green had grown weary of the discrimination Black people encountered whenever they went outside of their neighborhoods. Rates of car ownership had exploded around World War II (1939–1945), but interstate travel was risky for African Americans. This book was a tool to help Black travelers navigate in America. "Whites only" policies meant that Black travelers often could not find safe places to eat, sleep, get gas, or use the restroom in so-called "Sundown Towns." These types of towns banned Black people after dark and were scattered across the country, not only in the South.

In the 1956 edition of the Green Book, the foreword noted, "the White traveler has had no difficulty in getting accommodations, but with the Negro it has been different." The Green Book provided a list of hotels, gas stations, drug stores, barbershops, and restaurants that were known to be safe places for African American travelers.

The Green Book listed establishments in Southern segregated states, such as Alabama and Mississippi, but also included nontraditional segregated states from Connecticut to California. It listed any place where its readers might face discrimination or danger because of their skin color. With Jim Crow laws and culture affecting much of the country, a motto on the 1948 edition cover also served as a warning for the traveler: "Carry your Green Book with you—You may need it."

The Green Book reached around two million people during the early 1960s and also included international listings. The 1966-67 edition of the Green Book was the last to be published, as the need was thought to be diminished after the passing of the Civil Rights Act of 1964, which outlawed racial discrimination. However, racial discrimination and the threat of violence did not stop as a result of this law passing. Black people still had to be skilled and clever while traveling in America well after this publication ended. In fact, many Black Americans still take extreme caution when traveling throughout the United States in the Modern Day era.

GI BILL (1944–1956)

The *Servicemen's Readjustment Act of 1944* (also known as the *GI Bill*) was a law that provided a range of benefits for returning World War II (1939–1945) veterans. For Black veterans, the promise of the GI Bill turned out to be an illusion. Though the bill helped White veterans succeed and accrue wealth after the war, it did not deliver on that promise for Black veterans. In fact, the wide disparity in the bill's execution helped drive gaps in education, homeownership, and unemployment compensation between White and Black veterans. While the GI Bill's language did not explicitly deny benefits for Black veterans, its implementation excluded benefits to an estimated 1.2 million Black veterans, who had bravely served their country in segregated ranks.

When legislators began drafting the GI Bill, some Southern lawmakers feared that returning Black veterans would use public sympathy to dismantle Jim Crow segregation laws. To uphold the Jim Crow system and to make sure the GI Bill largely benefited White veterans, Southern lawmakers drew on tactics previously used and insisted the program be administered by individual states (states' rights) instead of the federal government. This gave power to local and state governments, as well as private stakeholders to execute the bill's benefits based on segregationist laws and culture, which proved discriminatory in most cases.

Black veterans had trouble securing the GI Bill's benefits from the beginning. In addition to the bill's biased execution, some Black veterans could not access benefits because they had not been given an honorable discharge. This tactic impacted a larger number of Black veterans compared to their White counterparts. Intimidation kept others from enjoying GI Bill benefits. For example, in 1947, a crowd threw rocks at Black veterans as they moved into a Chicago housing development. In the years following World War II, thousands of Black veterans were attacked and some were lynched.

Though the GI Bill guaranteed low-interest mortgages and other loans, they were not administered by the Veterans Administration (VA) itself. The VA could co-sign but not guarantee the loans, giving all White-run financial institutions complete authority to refuse mortgages and loans to Black people. As the years went on, White veterans flowed into newly created suburbs, where they began building wealth.

VA unemployment insurance was also administered unfairly. Black veterans who applied for unemployment benefits were kicked out of the program if any other work was available to them. This included work that provided considerably low wages. Some Southern mail carriers were even accused of refusing to deliver unemployment benefits applications to Black veterans.

Black veterans who pursued the GI Bill's education benefits fared no better. Many Black veterans returning home from the war did not apply for educational benefits, as they could not afford to spend time in school instead of working. However, those who did apply for educational benefits were at a significant disadvantage compared to their White counterparts. Public education provided poor preparation for Black students for higher education, as many Black schools were severely under-resourced compared to White schools. The VA encouraged most Black veterans to apply for occupational training programs instead of universities. Black veterans who did apply to universities often found themselves left out. Northern universities significantly delayed admitting Black students, and Southern White colleges denied Black students under Jim Crow laws. Although the GI Bill granted all soldiers the same benefits, discriminatory practices in higher education excluded most Black veterans from earning a college degree. Meanwhile, White veterans were being admitted into college, earning degrees, and creating wealth in professional positions.

Civil rights groups and Black veterans protested their treatment, but the racial disparities in the execution of the GI Bill had already taken effect. The original GI Bill ended in July 1956 and proved successful for many World War II veterans. It granted an estimated 4.3 million home loans worth thirty-three billion dollars and nearly eight million veterans received education or training. Most White veterans flourished but most Black veterans had been left behind. Preliminary analysis of historical data conducted by Maria Madison, director of the Institute for Economic and Racial Equity at Brandeis University, suggests Black and White veterans accessed their benefits at similar rates. However, due to the GI Bill's biased execution, Black veterans were more limited in the ways they could use their benefits. As a result, the cash equivalent for Black veteran benefits was only forty percent of what White veterans received. This difference in value equates to $170,000 less per Black veteran, after adjusting for inflation and market returns according to Madison.

The disparity in the GI Bill's benefits execution created wealth for White veterans, while widening existing disparities for their Black counterparts. According to historian Ira Katznelson, "There was no greater instrument for widening an already huge racial gap in postwar America than the GI Bill." The GI Bill's benefits were so prosperous for White people that some historians refer to this bill as affirmative action for White veterans and their families.

In the Modern Day era, a large wealth gap between Black and White Americans persists. According to the 2018 Current Population Survey (CPS) Annual Social and Economic Supplements (ASEC) conducted by the United States Census Bureau, Black families have a median household income of just over $41,000, whereas White families have a median household income of more than $70,000.

HOMEOWNERSHIP INJUSTICES

Newly freed Black people were denied land and homeownership as a result of broken promises such as those of the Freedmen's Bureau, the Forty Acres and a Mule order, and the immoral sharecropping system. However, the possibility of *homeownership* presented new opportunities for Black Americans beginning in the 1900s. The current homeownership system in the United States is primarily the result of the federal housing policies that were planned in the 1920s and executed during the 1930s.

The American Dream of homeownership was birthed during the Roaring Twenties (1920s) but was nearly crushed during the Great Depression (1930s). To rescue White homeowners from foreclosure, the government created the Home Owners' Loan Corporation (HOLC) in 1933. The HOLC refinanced delinquent mortgages with low-interest rates and long-term payment plans. While White people were avoiding foreclosure through HOLC policies, Black people were suffering foreclosure from these same policies, and "redlining" was a main offender. As a result, many Black Americans were excluded from homeownership which was directly tied to the 20th century's extraordinary economic gains.

Redlining was the practice of outlining neighborhoods by race on maps in all major cities in America. HOLC used this assessment to determine the risk levels of the mortgages it was buying. The "safest" neighborhoods were outlined in green and the "riskiest" neighborhoods were outlined in red. It was during this time that the national misconception that Black people were inherently violent and their presence in communities led to crime was intentionally crafted and spread. As a result, most neighborhoods in which Black Americans lived, received a red outline regardless of safety or economic prosperity.

The Federal Housing Administration (FHA) was created in 1934 to increase middle-class homeownership. It insured mortgages so that banks would increase the number of loans they issued. Adopting HOLC's racist risk assessment practices, redlining became an official requirement of FHA's federal mortgage insurance program. The practice of redlining was a huge success for many White families but excluded mostly everyone else. This practice ultimately prevented most Black Americans from accessing homeownership for many decades.

In addition to redlining, other strategies emerged within the housing industry to further exploit Black people seeking homeownership. Blockbusting and contract-buying were two of the most common practices.

Blockbusting was a scheme used to manipulate White homeowners into selling their homes for a discount by convincing them that Black people were moving into their neighborhoods. Oftentimes it was real estate speculators conducting this scheme. They hired Black people to spend time in White neighborhoods, then alert White homeowners that Black people were planning to purchase. Once a White homeowner on the block panicked and sold their home at a discount, the speculator would resell the home to a Black buyer at an inflated price. When the Black person moved in, other White homeowners sold their homes at discounted prices. This quickly shifted neighborhoods from White to Black at inflated prices, which caused home values to drop. The FHA then used declining home values in these newly created Black neighborhoods, as further evidence that its racist risk assessments were accurate.

As Black buyers became increasingly desperate to own homes, some became victims of contract-buying. In this scheme, Black home buyers were sold contracts that allowed them to live in a home, but not own it until the contract was paid in full. Most often, loopholes were used to take the home from Black home buyers before the end of the contract. Homeowners would sell housing contracts at inflated prices and then evict families unable to pay, keeping their down payment and monthly installments as profit. Then homeowners would bring in another Black family and repeat the scheme. Many Black families were determined to own homes and realized they had limited options, so they gravitated toward these high-risk contracts. According to Duke University's Samuel DuBois Cook Center on Social Equity, it is estimated that in Chicago alone, Black families lost between three to four billion dollars in wealth because of these types of predatory housing contracts in the 1950s and 1960s.

The usage of blockbusting and contract-buying demonstrates how speculators exploited White fear and Black determination for homeownership to profit at the expense of Black wealth. The Fair Housing Act of 1968, officially banned the practices of redlining, blockbusting, and contract-buying. However, this Act could not undo the decades of neighborhood segregation and Black financial disadvantage these practices caused. These practices, along with zoning laws, subprime lending, the discriminatory actions of the Department of Housing and Urban Development (HUD), and real estate unions are some of the reasons why most neighborhoods in America are still segregated today. Their deep effects have persisted for generations and have been a major driving force of the current racial wealth gap in the United States. Homeownership is a key indicator of wealth and can be passed down and/or sold contributing to economic gains and generational wealth.

According to the United States Chamber of Commerce, in 2016, the median net worth of a White family was $171,000, whereas the median net worth of a Black family was $17,150—approximately ten times less. Nearly a century of low homeownership in the Black community is one of the biggest culprits for the racial wealth gap.

AMERICAN FEDERALISM (STATES' RIGHTS VS. FEDERAL AUTHORITY)

A merican Federalism is the system of government in which the same geographic location is controlled by both the federal and state governments. It grants certain powers to each of the two levels of government. While it was important to the framers of the American Constitution to separate governmental power, federalism has also been a continual source of contention between the two levels of government.

The rights granted to the federal government are enumerated in the Constitution, giving the United States Congress certain exclusive powers, such as the ability to declare war, coin money, and control interstate commerce. Under the Tenth Amendment, ratified in 1791, powers not specifically listed in the Constitution are reserved to the states, such as the ability to regulate policing, running of elections, education, marriage, and intrastate trade. There are also shared powers between the federal government and the states, including the ability to tax, borrow money, and legislate.

The line between the powers of the United States federal government and those of the states is usually clear, but not always. When a state's government exercise of power conflicts with the Constitution, there is a battle for "states' rights" which most often is settled by the United States Supreme Court. When there is a conflict between a state and a similar federal law, according to the Supremacy Clause found in Article VI, the federal law supersedes state law only if it does not conflict with the Constitution.

States' rights have been used to create many racist systems in the United States, which had damaging effects for Black people. Southern states seceded from the Union prior to the Civil War in part because they believed the federal government was unconstitutionally infringing on their states' rights in regards to the institution of Chattel Slavery. After Reconstruction, Southern states used states' rights to adopt new state constitutions and enacted laws that raised barriers to Black voter participation. This resulted in most Black voters being disenfranchised by poll taxes, discriminatory literacy tests, and other barriers to voting. With the Black vote suppressed, Southern states were legally able to pass racist Jim Crow laws, which lasted roughly a hundred years.

In the 1950s and 1960s, the Civil Rights Movement successfully challenged the racist Jim Crow laws enacted in Southern states. This increased pressure on the federal government to protect the voting rights of racial minorities. Federal authority powers led to monumental laws being passed during the Civil Rights Movement, overturning racist Jim Crow laws. This did not occur without a battle; Southern states argued their states' rights had been violated, and many times the federal government had to intervene. The National Guard was sometimes deployed to ensure states followed the new civil rights laws and to protect Black citizens while desegregating the South.

States' rights were used to justify Chattel Slavery and Jim Crow, and this strategy is still used by Congress in the Modern Day era. It is not uncommon for legislators to invoke the states' rights argument when debating controversial issues such as COVID-19 mask mandates, immigration, gun rights, and abortion.

CIVIL RIGHTS MOVEMENT (1954–1968)

The *Civil Rights Movement* of the 1950s and 1960s emerged from the need and desire of Black Americans to gain equal rights and freedom. Nearly a hundred years after Chattel Slavery was abolished, there were widespread Jim Crow laws that legalized segregation, discrimination, and disenfranchisement for Black people. These laws, along with racially motivated violence, impacted the personal and structural aspects of life for Southern Black people. It was during this period the Democratic Party took up the mantle of civil rights and the majority of Black support shifted from Republican to Democrat.

During the Civil Rights Movement, there was a big surge of activism taking place to reverse segregation, injustice, and discrimination. Activists worked together and famously used non-violent tactics and civil disobedience to peacefully challenge unfair laws. They used strategies like boycotts, sit-ins, and protest marches in their effort to desegregate the South. Often police or racist White people would attack them, but the activists did not fight back.

The Civil Rights Movement increased pressure on the federal government to protect the civil and voting rights of racial minorities. Many credit the Montgomery Bus Boycott inspired by Rosa Parks as the catalyst that began this movement. This era produced many civil rights leaders, most notably Dr. Martin Luther King, Jr. As a result of the courageous civil rights activists, landmark civil rights legislation was passed between 1954 and 1968. During this relatively short period of time, fundamental change was made, and its impact can be seen in our society today.

The Civil Rights Movement was very successful. As a result, ground-breaking and sweeping civil rights laws were passed including *Brown v. Board of Education* in 1954, which desegregated public schools, and the Civil Rights Act of 1957, which authorized federal prosecution of anyone attempting to prevent someone from voting. It also created the Civil Rights Division within the Department of Justice to enforce civil rights through court proceedings and created the Commission on Civil Rights to investigate voting rights injustices. Further protections were enacted in the Civil Rights Act of 1960, which established federal inspection of local voter registration polls and imposed penalties for violators.

The Civil Rights Act of 1964 overruled Jim Crow laws, prohibiting segregation in public places and making employment discrimination illegal based on race, color, religion, sex, or national origin. This Act was the most extensive civil rights legislation passed since the Reconstruction era. When the Voting Rights Act of 1965 passed, this legislation protected minority voting rights, banning states from passing discriminatory laws and requiring certain state and local governments to get federal approval before making any changes to their voting laws or procedures. The Civil Rights Act of 1968 was passed as an expansion of the Civil Rights Act of 1964. Title VIII of the Civil Rights Act of 1968, commonly known as the "Fair Housing Act," prohibited housing discrimination making it illegal to interfere with housing rights and opportunities regardless of race, creed, or national origin.

These Acts "ended" this dark time in American history. It also helped change many White Americans' attitudes about the way Black people were treated and the rights they deserved.

Black Americans have had to fight for every right they have gained. This fight continues in the Modern Day era and will continue as long as inequality between races exists. Segregation is no longer legal in the United States; however, many schools, neighborhoods, churches, and other places are still profoundly segregated to this day. This is known as de facto segregation.

COINTELPRO (1956–1971)

C OINTELPRO (a syllabic abbreviation derived from COunter INTELligence PROgram) was a series of secret and unlawful projects conducted by the United States Federal Bureau of Investigation (FBI) from 1956 to 1971. The goal of this program was to discredit and neutralize "radical" American political organizations. The FBI conducted COINTELPRO operations by spying on, infiltrating, discrediting, and disrupting targeted individuals and organizations. According to a Senate report, the FBI's motivation was "protecting national security, preventing violence, and maintaining the existing social and political order by 'disrupting' and 'neutralizing' groups and individuals perceived as threats."

The FBI had used secret operations against domestic political groups since its founding in 1908; however, covert operations under the official COINTELPRO label took place between 1956 and 1971. This specific government program was used to target and destroy civil rights organizations and leaders. The first FBI director, J. Edgar Hoover, approved the FBI's ongoing surveillance of Black leaders using the COINTELPRO program with the false justification that the movement was infiltrated by communists. Some of the notable targets were Dr. Martin Luther King, Jr., Malcolm X, and the Black Panther Party.

After the March on Washington in 1963, Dr. Martin Luther King, Jr. was considered the "most dangerous Negro" in the United States and singled out as a major target of COINTELPRO. The FBI wiretapped Dr. King's home and hotel rooms, and even tried to blackmail him into committing suicide. In the mid-1960s, Dr. King began to publicly criticize the FBI for giving insufficient attention to domestic terrorism conducted by White supremacists. Hoover responded by publicly calling Dr. King the most "notorious liar" in the United States. During the same time period, the program also targeted Malcolm X. It is documented that the FBI worked to further erode his relationship with Elijah Muhammad (his former mentor and teacher) by fostering internal disputes. These disputes ultimately led to Malcolm X's assassination in 1965 (the FBI, however, is not directly linked to his murder). Leaders and members of the Black Panther Party were also targeted by COINTELPRO and "neutralized" by many tactics such as assassination, imprisonment, and public humiliation.

In 1967, the FBI began "COINTELPRO–Black Hate." The program's goal was to stop Black Nationalist organizations from unifying and creating a Black "messiah" to lead them. This program focused on groups such as the Southern Christian Leadership Conference, the Student Nonviolent Coordinating Committee, and the Nation of Islam. Black Hate famously established the Ghetto Informant Program that instructed twenty-three FBI offices to conduct intelligence gathering operations.

COINTELPRO was secret until 1971, when the Citizens' Commission to Investigate the FBI broke into an FBI field office in Media, Pennsylvania. Commission members took several records and exposed the program by giving these materials to news agencies. That same year, Director J. Edgar Hoover announced that the COINTELPRO program was over and that all future counterintelligence operations would be handled on an individual basis.

The FBI did little to discourage or shut down the injustices, laws, and domestic terrorism that created the need for the Civil Rights Movement; instead, they targeted civil rights leaders and organizations as threats to democracy. Programs such as COINTELPRO and other FBI actions are why some Black Americans are suspicious of law enforcement and the FBI in the Modern Day era.

VOTING RIGHTS ACT (1965)

S ince the end of the Reconstruction era in 1877, Southern states have actively passed laws and used many tactics to keep Black Americans from exercising their right to vote. Examples of these tactics include grandfather clauses (laws that restricted voting rights to people whose forefathers had voted before the Civil War), poll taxes (fees charged to vote), White primaries (only White Democrats could vote), and literacy tests (unrealistic tests to vote, which in some instances required the registrant to name all the vice presidents and Supreme Court justices throughout America's history). Often, these laws did not apply to White Americans. The infamous *Plessy v. Ferguson* case in 1896 made racial segregation legal and solidified the message that discrimination against Black Americans was acceptable. When Black people attempted to vote, they were often met with violence. The police, the Ku Klux Klan, and White racists often beat, arrested, and sometimes murdered them.

As a result of the courageous civil rights activists, the *Voting Rights Act* was signed into law on August 6, 1965. This law made it illegal to stop someone from voting because of their race. This meant that all state laws that kept Black people from voting were now illegal. It also required certain state and local governments with a history of voting discrimination to get approval from the federal government before making any changes to their voting laws or procedures. Prior to this law, local registrars had total power over who they would and would not register to vote. If a registrar refused to let a Black person register to vote, that person could only file a lawsuit, which they were not likely to win, as the criminal justice system was primarily comprised of White people during Jim Crow. However, the Voting Rights Act finally made a change to this system. If local registrars discriminated against Black people, the Attorney General could send federal workers to replace them. The law worked right away and within a few months, approximately 250,000 Black Americans had newly registered to vote. One out of every three new Black voters were registered by a federal worker who replaced a local racist registrar. By 1967, most African Americans were registered to vote in nine of the thirteen Southern states.

Politics in the South were completely changed by Black Americans having the power to vote. White politicians could no longer make laws that impact Black Americans without their say in the voting booth. In some parts of the South, Black people outnumbered White people. This meant they could vote in Black politicians and vote out racist White politicians. Mississippi was a successful example of how Black voters changed the state's political landscape. In 1964 only 6.7 percent of eligible Black voters in Mississippi were registered to vote, by 1967 that number had increased to 59.8 percent. Black Mississippians used their newfound voting power to elect the most Black office holders of any Southern state by 1972. Also, Black people who were registered to vote could be on juries. Before this, any time a Black American was charged with a crime, the jury that decided their guilt or innocence would be all White. Black people had not had this type of voting power since the Reconstruction era, a hundred years earlier.

PART 4

MODERN DAY ERA (1968–PRESENT)

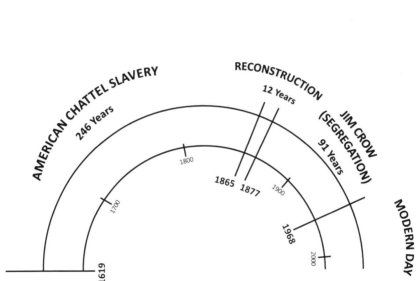

MODERN DAY (1968–PRESENT)

B lack Americans entered the *Modern Day* era with some cautious optimism, given the progress made over the previous generation. Black Americans have made lasting contributions to American history and culture, despite the unprecedented brutality and injustices (many legal) they faced for over 400 hundred years during Chattel Slavery, the Reconstruction era, Jim Crow, the Civil Rights Movement, and beyond.

Though issues of discrimination remain, Black Americans endure, achieve, and lead. Black Americans have made and continue to make monumental contributions to every part of American society including television and film (Oprah Winfrey), literature (Toni Morrison), music (Michael Jackson), sports (Jackie Robinson), medicine (Ben Carson), entrepreneurship (Robert L. Johnson), and politics (election and re-election of Barack Obama as the 44th President of the United States), just to name a few.

Despite all of this success, Black Americans still find themselves facing similar obstacles today as those faced by past generations. With the rise of the Black elite, a clear gap now separates the Black middle and small upper class from those living in poverty. Overall, Black communities continue to face systemic racism, police violence, mass incarceration, new voter suppression tactics, drug infiltration, and disparities in education, housing, healthcare, and other aspects of life.

In an era when Black Americans prominently influence American cultural and political affairs, social justice and racial equity remain coveted goals rather than accomplishments. The fight for equality continues with new tools, such as social media and video-recording smartphones, to document and comment on history in the making.

MODERN DAY ERA VOTER SUPPRESSION TACTICS

A healthy and successful democracy requires the full participation of all its citizens. By this definition, America's democracy has not been healthy or successful. Throughout history, many of her Black citizens have not been able to fully participate in the democratic process. This led to racist laws being passed, including those under the Jim Crow system. This happened as a result of the Black vote being suppressed and Black lawmakers being largely nonexistent for most of America's history. Today, many Black Americans are still facing *Modern Day era voter suppression tactics.*

Since the ending of the Civil Rights Movement in 1968, the number of Black Americans elected to the United States Congress has dramatically increased. Still, it was not until 2019, more than half a century later, that the share of Black members serving in the House of Representatives reached twelve percent, closely reflecting the percentage of Black Americans in the total population. As of January 2021, only eleven Black senators from seven states have ever been elected or appointed in United States history (there was another Black senator elected in the 1870s, but his election was successfully contested and his opponent took office instead). Unfortunately, many states have never elected a Black legislator to either chamber of Congress. Kamala Harris made history as the only Black vice president (also first woman and first person of South Asian descent), and Barack Obama is the only Black American to serve as president in the history of the United States.

History has shown that Black voter suppression was very effective in states passing racist laws. This has caused unprecedented damage to Black Americans and has contributed to the many disparities seen in the Black community today in areas such as healthcare, housing, education, and wealth. Despite legal and policy advancements that have extended the right to vote, the United States continues to invoke the ghosts of an ugly past by deploying new voter suppression tactics that target Black Americans and other people of color, in the Modern Day era.

In recent years, policymakers have tested the limits of how far they can go to prevent people of color from voting. Discriminatory voter purges, gerrymandering, modern day poll taxes, and the denial of citizenship threaten to overturn American democracy. In 2013, the United States Supreme Court's decision gutted Section 5 of the Voting Rights Act in *Shelby County v. Holder* by declaring the formula used to determine covered jurisdictions unconstitutional. Without a coverage formula, Section 5 is virtually unenforceable, allowing states with a history of voter suppression once again the ability to manipulate their voting policies and procedures without first seeking approval from federal officials. In 2018, the United States Supreme Court again gave voter suppression another victory with its ruling in *Husted v. A. Philip Randolph Institute*. The Supreme Court's decision upheld Ohio's practice of removing eligible voters from voter rolls for infrequent voting over a six-year period. This practice is known as purging and disproportionately impacted Ohio's Black voters. The *Husted* decision opened the door for other states to adopt similar practices, which could result in millions of Americans of color being removed from voter rolls.

As evidenced in the 2020 Presidential election, Black voter suppressors were right all along: Black votes are powerful. Black voters were pivotal to victory for the historic Biden-Harris ticket. It was the Black vote that swayed the election in Michigan, Pennsylvania, Wisconsin, and Georgia, not to mention the Black vote in South Carolina jump-started Joe Biden's path to victory.

Since then, we have seen many attempts of modern day voter suppression tactics including the Trump Administration's frivolous lawsuits challenging votes in predominantly Black areas. Reminiscent of the Ku Klux Klan's past intimidation tactics, an angry mostly White mob stormed into and vandalized the United States Capitol building on January 6, 2021. These actions were in support of President Donald Trump's attempts to overturn the 2020 presidential election. The result was massive property damage, numerous bodily injuries, and even deaths. The lesson of the 2020 presidential election is that the Black vote is powerful. Black Americans should continue to exercise their right to vote in order to influence legislation that will positively impact Black Americans at the national, state, and local levels.

Remaining vigilant against voter suppression efforts and rejecting all remnants of the racist past is not an option, but a necessity to protect America's democracy. It is abundantly clear that Black Americans are still fighting to obtain equal rights and will need to keep fighting as long as inequality exists.

AFFIRMATIVE ACTION

B eginning in the 1960s, the term "*affirmative action*" was used to refer to policies and initiatives that tried to remedy the effects of historical racial discrimination by assuring present opportunities for Black Americans. President John F. Kennedy first used the phrase in 1961, in Executive Order 10925 requiring federal contractors to "take affirmative action to ensure that applicants are employed, and that employees are treated during employment, without regard to their race, creed, color, or national origin." In the late 1960s, gender was added to the anti-discrimination list. Executive Order 10925 was the precursor to subsequent affirmative action programs.

Affirmative action programs helped increase educational and employment opportunities for some African Americans, paving the way for them to climb into the middle and upper-middle classes. Sometimes quota systems were used in school admission and job hiring, which led to accusations of reverse discrimination by some non-minorities.

In the mid-1970s, many universities were seeking to increase the minority and female, faculty and student population on their campuses. For example, the University of California, Davis (UC Davis), reserved sixteen percent of its medical school's admissions spots for minority applicants. Allan Bakke, a White California man, was denied admission twice and sued UC Davis, claiming "reverse discrimination." He claimed his grades and test scores were higher than those of minority students who were admitted. In 1978, his landmark case, *Regents of the University of California v. Bakke*, was decided by the United States Supreme Court. The Supreme Court ruled that the use of strict racial quotas was unconstitutional and that Bakke should be admitted. Ironically, it also ruled that institutions of higher education could rightfully use race as a criterion for college admissions to ensure diversity.

After the *Bakke* verdict, affirmative action continued to be a controversial and divisive issue, with growing resistance. Opponents claimed the so-called "racial playing field" was now equal and that Black Americans no longer needed special consideration. In rulings over the next decades, the courts limited the scope of affirmative action programs. Several states completely eliminated race-based affirmative action altogether. As affirmative action was being rolled back on race, it proved successful for other protected classes, such as gender, and has historically provided great benefits to White women. According to a 1995 Department of Labor report, there are at least six million women—the majority of them White—who would not have their current jobs but for affirmative action. Research shows that one of the greatest beneficiaries of affirmative action over the last forty years is White women, especially in higher education.

CRACK EPIDEMIC (1980s–1990s)

The "*Crack Epidemic*" in the United States happened in major cities across America in the 1980s and 1990s. Crack is a cheaper alternative to powder cocaine, and its affordability made it more accessible in low-income, predominately Black neighborhoods. As a result, it had particularly devastating effects within the Black community, causing an increase in substance abuse, deaths, and drug-related crimes. Entire communities were shattered, and tough crime policies were established, leading to mass incarceration.

Crack production began in the 1980s, and unlike powder cocaine, crack was easy to develop and cheaper to buy. San Jose Mercury News journalist Gary Webb alleged in his 1996 Dark Alliance series that the Central Intelligence Agency (CIA) of the United States was partially responsible for bringing crack cocaine to the United States in the 1980s. In 1998, a CIA inspector general's report denied any relationship between the United States government and the drug dealers that Webb indicated in his series. However, the CIA ultimately confirmed Webb's theory that they had worked with contras despite drug-dealing allegations against them. To this day, it is widely believed by many in the Black community that the government did infiltrate Black neighborhoods with crack to intentionally tear down Black families and communities.

The arrival of crack cocaine in the inner cities created a drastic increase in crime between 1981 and 1986. Drug offenses and drug-related crimes such as murders, robberies, and aggravated assaults significantly increased federal prison admissions. In an effort to combat the crack epidemic, the Anti-Drug Abuse Act was signed into law in 1986 by President Ronald Reagan.

The Anti-Drug Abuse Act of 1986 created huge disparities in sentencing between crack and powder cocaine. Under this bill, an offender received a five-year minimum sentence for five grams of crack cocaine, but it took 500 grams of powder cocaine to receive the same sentence—a ratio of 100:1. To justify sentence disparities, some argue that crack cocaine is more addictive and therefore deserves a higher sentence. However, many medical experts dispute this claim, stating there is no pathological difference between the two forms of cocaine. Many people believe that because crack cocaine is statistically linked to impoverished Black communities, while powder cocaine use is most common among affluent White communities, the legal disparity between powder and crack cocaine is rooted in racism.

The Anti-Drug Abuse Act of 1986 focused on small-time drug dealers, who were largely poor young Black males from inner cities. The prison population ultimately doubled due to the arrest of drug dealers and their customers. One in every four African American males aged 20 to 29 was either incarcerated, on probation, or on parole by 1989. This contributed to the United States having the highest incarceration rate in the world. By 1995, the incarceration rate of Black males aged 20 to 29 increased to nearly one in three. In 2010, President Barack Obama signed into law the Fair Sentencing Act. This law reduced the crack/powder cocaine disparity from 100:1 to 18:1. Although this effort was needed, it was also considered too little, too late as the damage had already been done within the Black community, and its effects continue to this day.

Currently, in the Modern Day era, America is experiencing an opioid crisis that is primarily affecting the White community, which accounts for roughly eighty percent of opioid overdose victims. The opioid crisis is classified as a public health emergency where addicts are treated as patients and given treatment. In contrast, the crack epidemic was classified as a war on drugs where addicts were treated as criminals and incarcerated. Due to the racial disparity between Black people (crack) and White people (opioids), many people believe this is an example of race once again being used to criminalize Black people.

DE FACTO SEGREGATION

When Dr. Martin Luther King, Jr. delivered his "I Have a Dream" speech on August 28, 1963, during the March on Washington, he called for an end to segregation and issued a plea for equality and freedom for African Americans. This speech, along with the nonviolent tactics of the Civil Rights Movement, produced many legal gains for racial equality including the Civil Rights Act of 1964, the Voting Rights Act of 1965, and the Fair Housing Act of 1968. These laws put an end to the racist legal systems during Jim Crow, but Dr. King's dream of equality is still not fully realized today.

More than half a century after Dr. King's speech and the end of the Civil Rights Movement, racial segregation still plagues America. When we look at contemporary racial segregation, we must consider it through a *de facto segregation* lens. According to the Merriam-Webster dictionary, de facto segregation stems "from economic or social factors rather than from laws or actions of the state." In other words, de facto segregation is the separation of groups because of past systems, facts, circumstances, customs, or personal choices. Although it is appropriate to celebrate the many racial equality gains won throughout history, we must also understand how de facto segregation continues to separate and create inequities in America's institutions

Racial segregation is obvious in residential neighborhoods, but it impacts all of America's institutions, such as the federal government, healthcare, education, criminal justice, business management, and religion. Below are impacts of de facto segregation in the Modern Day era:

- Federal government: 2019 was the first year that the number of Black members serving in the U.S. House of Representatives closely reflected the population of Black Americans (roughly twelve percent).

- Education: Schools remain segregated as Black students are twice as likely to attend high-poverty schools as their White peers; only 8.4 percent of White students attend high-poverty, non-White schools compared to sixty percent of Black students.

- Wealth: In 2016, the median net worth of a White family was $171,000, whereas the median net worth of a Black household was $17,150 (ten times less).

- Healthcare: Race is associated with access-to-care disparities, with Black Americans adversely and disproportionately impacted by poor access to healthcare.

- Criminal justice: Black Americans represent forty percent of the incarcerated population, and Black Americans are incarcerated in state prisons at 5.1 times the rate of White Americans.

- High-level management positions: In 2019, Black American representation was 8.9 percent in "high earning management and professional" roles, less than their roughly twelve percent workforce representation.

- Religion: A 2014 study showed Sunday morning remains one of the most segregated hours in American life, with more than eight in ten congregations made up of one predominant racial group. Only about a third (thirty-four percent) of Americans have regularly attended a house of worship where they were a minority.

These facts are not a comprehensive list as many more American institutions have racial disparities. However, the facts listed above make it evident that America still has a lot of work to do to end segregation.

ACKNOWLEDGEMENTS

Thank you God for the many blessings
you have bestowed upon me, every day of my life!
— Ephesians 3:20 and Jeremiah 29:11

There are so many people I'd like to thank for their support, too many to name everyone. To my parents (James Bruce and Mary Ray Bruce), grandparents (Sim & Albirda Ray and Willie & Mary Bruce Jr.), family, and friends who know about my Black history passion—thanks for your extreme excitement for me and this project! Special shout out to Danny L. Lambouths III, I can't thank you enough for writing my foreword. You all have affirmed this book and offered support in many ways! I fully recognize that I have a village who has positively contributed to every aspect of my life, in all seasons of my life. I thank God for you all and recognize your presence in my life as a gift of His amazing love, grace, and mercy.
I am extremely blessed and grateful!

To my sisters, Tamara Bruce Williams and Tashica Bruce, who are both bosses and pushed me to become one as well! I had to do something to keep up. ☺ You both helped me realize this book is a natural extension of my God-given passion. You both helped me realize I needed to share my gift and get this book out, even with extreme reluctance. You both helped me realize that I was born for this very purpose and I can never repay you for that! I'm not sure I have the words to express my gratitude, but I am extremely thankful!

And to my sister/cousin, Nefiteria Ray, who is also a boss and makes big things happen! I often feel like you're my personal cheerleader. You are a natural encourager who always has my back and is always down for anything. I thank you for always believing in me. I hope that I play a similar role in your life!

Writing a book was never a dream of mine and the process has been extremely painful. I don't have any natural children yet, but feel like I birthed this book. Two of my best friends, Satara McMillian and Tiffany Jackson, have been my midwives during this process and relentlessly forced me to push until I delivered this book. There were many times when I wanted to stop, but they helped soothe and reassure me when I felt the pain and weight of this project was too much to bear. They held me accountable and basically forced me into completion. Without their "tough love," this project may have never come into fruition. I felt bruised and mentally drained many days, but thank you for your continued persistence in driving me to complete this project. I am amazed by your confidence in me!

I love you all!!!

I would also like to give a special thank you to Alex Bland, the amazing artist who created the Black Liberty image on my book cover. He graciously allowed me (a person he's never met) to use his powerful and beautiful masterpiece for my book cover, and I am extremely grateful. Please check out Alex's amazing body of work at www.alexbland.com.

ENDNOTES

Front Cover Image

Bland, A. Cover Image. *Black Liberty*. www.alexbland.com

#1 Transatlantic Slave Trade/Middle Passage (1500s–1870s)

DeGruy, J.A. (2017). *Post Traumatic Slave Syndrome: America's Legacy of Enduring Injury and Healing* (Revised ed.). Joy DeGruy Publications Incorporated. pp. 33-35, 57-58. ISBN 978-0985217273.

Ivanova, K. (2020, June 11). *The Terrifying Conditions Aboard a Slave Ship*. I Intelligence. com. https://iheartintelligence.com/the-terrifying-conditions-aboard-a-slave-ship/

Mancke, E. & Shammas, C (2005). *The Creation of the British Atlantic World*. Johns Hopkins University Press. pp. 30–31.

Middle Passage | Definition, Conditions, Significance, & Facts. (n.d.). Encyclopedia Britannica. https://www.britannica.com/topic/Middle-Passage-slave-trade

Muhammad, P.M. (2003). *The Trans-Atlantic Slave Trade: A Forgotten Crime Against Humanity as Defined by International Law*. American University International Law Review, 19 (4).

Slave Ship Mutinies. (n.d.) Slavery and Remembrance. http://slaveryandremembrance.org/articles/article/?id=A0035

The 1619 Project. (2019, August 18). The New York Times Magazine. https://www.nytimes.com/interactive/2019/08/14/magazine/1619-america-slavery.html

Understanding Slavery Initiative. (n.d.) Understanding Slavery Initiative. http://www.understandingslavery.com/

#2 Religion

Boney, J. L. (2018, June 27). *Do You Recognize This America? Using Religion to Justify Racism*. Houston Forward Times. https://forwardtimes.com/do-you-recognize-this-america-using-religion-to-justify-racism/

Dallas, K. (2019, August 29). *Why understanding the relationship between Christianity and slavery is 'hard, soul-shaking work.'* Deseret News. https://www.deseret.com/indepth/2019/8/28/20833722/americans-religion-and-slavery-racism-abolition-race-faith

Devitt, J. (2020 February 3). *"The Reckoning is Real": On Slavery, the Church, and How Some 21st-Centruy Institutions Are (Finally) Starting to Talk About Reparations*. New York University. https://www.nyu.edu/about/news-publications/news/2020/february/-the-reckoning-is-real---on-slavery--the-church--and-how-some-21.html

Gjelten, T. (2020, July 1). *White Supremacist Ideas Have Historic Roots in U.S. Christianity*. NPR.org. https://www.npr.org/2020/07/01/883115867/white-supremacist-ideas-have-historical-roots-in-u-s-christianity

Johnson, A. E. (2017, August 29). *Henry McNeal Turner: Church Planter, Politician, and Public Theologian*. Christian History | Learn the History of Christianity & the Church. https://www.christianitytoday.com/history/2017/september/henry-mcneal-turner-church-planter-politician-and-public-th.html

Jones, R.P. (2020, July 28). *Racism among white Christians is higher than among the nonreligious. That's no coincidence*. NBC News. https://www.nbcnews.com/think/opinion/racism-among-white-christians-higher-among-nonreligious-s-no-coincidence-ncna1235045

Singh, S. J. (2020, July 9). *To fight racism, we need to confront religion's racist past*. Religion News Service. https://religionnews.com/2020/07/09/how-americas-religious-colonizers-brought-racism-with-them/

The Black Church In America, a story. (2021, November 1). African American Registry. https://aaregistry.org/story/the-black-church-a-brief-history/

The Slave Experience: Religion. Thirteen.org. https://www.thirteen.org/wnet/slavery/experience/religion/history2.html

Weil, J. Z. (2019, April 30). *The Bible was used to justify slavery. Then Africans made it their path to freedom*. Washington Post. https://www.washingtonpost.com/local/the-bible-was-used-to-justify-slavery-then-africans-made-it-their-path-to-freedom/2019/04/29/34699e8e-6512-11e9-82ba-fcfeff232e8f_story.html

Williams, S.D. (2020, June15). *The church must make reparation for its role in slavery, segregation*. National Catholic Reporter. https://www.ncronline.org/news/opinion/church-must-make-reparation-its-role-slavery-segregation

#3 1619

Austin, Beth (August 2019). *"1619: Virginia's First Africans"*. Hampton History Museum.

Brown, D. L. (2018, August 24). *Slavery's bitter roots: In 1619, '20 And odd Negroes' arrived in Virginia*. Washington Post. https://www.washingtonpost.com/news/retropolis/wp/2018/08/24/slaverys-bitter-roots-in-1619-20-and-odd-negroes-arrived-in-virginia/

History.com Editors. (2021, August 23). *Slavery in America*. HISTORY. https://www.history.com/topics/black-history/slavery

Petras, G., Padilla, R., Hao, S., Sneed, S., Sergent, J., Sullivan, S., Thorson, M., Zarracina, J., & Nichols, M. (n.d.) *Slavery's explosive growth, in charts: How '20 and odd' became millions*. USA Today. https://www.usatoday.com/pages/interactives/1619-african-slavery-history-maps-routes-interactive-graphic/?utm_source=oembed&utm_medium=onsite&utm_campaign=s2seriesrecirc&utm_content=news

Shipp, E. (2019, February 9). *1619: 400 years ago, a ship arrived in Virginia, bearing human cargo*. USA TODAY. https://www.usatoday.com/story/news/investigations/2019/02/08/1619-african-arrival-virginia/2740468002/

The 1619 Project. (2019, August 18). The New York Times Magazine. https://www.nytimes.com/interactive/2019/08/14/magazine/1619-america-slavery.html

Waxman, O.B. (2019, August 20). *The First Africans in Virginia Landed in 1619. It Was a Turning Point for Slavery in American History—But Not the Beginning.* Time. https://time.com/5653369/august-1619-jamestown-history/

#4 Chattel Slavery (1619–1865)

A Brief History of Civil Rights in the United States. Georgetown Law Library. https://guides.ll.georgetown.edu/c.php?g=592919&p=4100954

Definition of chattel slavery. (n.d.) Dictionary.com. https://www.dictionary.com/browse/chattel-slavery

DeGruy, J.A. (2017). *Post Traumatic Slave Syndrome: America's Legacy of Enduring Injury and Healing* (Revised ed.). Joy DeGruy Publications Incorporated. pp. 33-35, 57-58. ISBN 978-0985217273.

History.com Editors. (2021, August 23). *Slavery in America.* HISTORY. https://www.history.com/topics/black-history/slavery

Indentured Servants (n.d.). Ushistory.org. https://www.ushistory.org/us/5b.asp

Kane, B. (2020, March). *Top 10 Horrible Punishments for Slaves in America.* ListVerse. https://listverse.com/2020/03/01/top-10-horrible-punishments-for-slaves-in-america/

Ross, J. (2019, July 10). *As McConnell's family shows, the legacy of slavery persists in most American lives.* NBC News. https://www.nbcnews.com/news/nbcblk/mcconnell-s-family-shows-legacy-slavery-persists-most-american-lives-n1028031

The 1619 Project. (2019, August 18). The New York Times Magazine. https://www.nytimes.com/interactive/2019/08/14/magazine/1619-america-slavery.html

Thomas, Z. (2019, August 29). *The hidden links between slavery and Wall Street.* BBC News. https://www.bbc.com/news/business-49476247

#5 Race Factored into Law (1600s)

Africans in America/Part 1/Bacon's Rebellion. (n.d.). PBS. https://www.pbs.org/wgbh/aia/part1/1p274.html

Donoghue, J. (2010). Out of the Land of Bondage: The English Revolution and the Atlantic Origins of Abolition". *The American Historical Review. 115 (4), 943-974.* https://doi.org/10.1086/ahr.115.4.943

Finkelman, P. (1985). *Slavery in the Courtroom: An Annotated Bibliography of American Cases.* Library of Congress. ISBN 978-1886363489.

Foner, E. (2009). *Give Me Liberty!: An American History.* W.W. Norton & Company, p. 100.

Green Spring Plantation. Historic Jamestowne, National Park Service.

Morgan, E. S. (1975). *American Slavery, American Freedom: The Ordeal of Colonial Virginia. (1st ed).* W.W. Norton & Company, Inc.

The 1619 Project. (2019, August 18). The New York Times Magazine. https://www.nytimes.com/interactive/2019/08/14/magazine/1619-america-slavery.html

Virginia Slave Laws. (n.d.) Digital History. https://www.digitalhistory.uh.edu/disp_textbook.cfm?smtID=3&psid=71

#6 Slave Codes (1691)

African Americans—The Civil War era. (n.d.). Encyclopedia Britannica. https://www.britannica.com/topic/African-American/The-Civil-War-era

Barbadians in Carolina. (n.d.) The Lowcountry Digital History Initiative. https://ldhi.library.cofc.edu/exhibits/show/africanpassageslowcountryadapt/sectionii_introduction/barbadians_in_carolina

Blackmon, D. (2008). *Slavery by Another Name: The Re-Enslavement of Black Americans from the Civil War to World War II.* New York: Doubleday.

Charleston County Public Library. (2021, August 27). *Escaping Slavery: Resistance on the Run.* https://www.ccpl.org/charleston-time-machine/escaping-slavery-resistance-run

Forehand, B. (1996). *Striking Resemblance: Kentucky, Tennessee, Black Codes and Readjustment, 1865-1866.* pp. 6-7.

Forte, D. F. (1998). *Spiritual Equality, the Black Codes, and the Americanization of the Freedmen.* 43 Loyola Law Review 569. pp. 579–580.

Gates, H. L. (n.d.). *Free Blacks Lived in the North, Right?.* The African Americans: Many Rivers to Cross. PBS. Originally posted on The Root. https://www.pbs.org/wnet/african-americans-many-rivers-to-cross/history/free-blacks-lived-in-the-north-right/

History.com Editors. (2021a, January 21). *Black Codes.* HISTORY. https://www.history.com/topics/black-history/black-codes

Painter, N. I. (2006). Creating Black Americans: *African-American History and Its Meanings, 1619 to the Present* (Illustrated ed.). Oxford University Press. pp. 79–81.

Ranney, J. A. (2006). *In the Wake of Slavery: Civil War, Civil Rights, and the Reconstruction of Southern Law* (Illustrated ed.). Praeger. p. 15

Rugemer, E. B. (2013). *The Development of Mastery and Race in the Comprehensive Slave Codes of the Greater Caribbean during the Seventeenth Century.* The William and Mary Quarterly. 70 (3): 429–458. www.JSTOR.org/stable/10.5309/willmaryquar.70.3.0429.

Rugemer, E. B. (2018). *Slave Law and the Politics of Resistance in the Early Atlantic World.* Harvard University Press. https://brill.com/view/journals/nwig/94/1-2/article-p113_5.xml?language=en

#7 Slave Patrols (1704)

Bellesiles, M. (1999, March). *Lethal Imagination: Violence and Brutality in American History.* NYU Press; Edition Unstated edition. Print.

Douglass, F. (1995). *Narrative of the Life of Frederick Douglass.* New York Dover Publications.

Hassett-Walker, C. (2021, January 11). *How You Start is How You Finish? The Slave Patrol and Jim Crow Origins of Policing.* American Bar Association. https://www.americanbar.org/groups/crsj/publications/human_rights_magazine_home/civil-rights-reimagining-policing/how-you-start-is-how-you-finish/

Slave Patrols: An Early Form of American Policing. (2021, August 18). National Law Enforcement Officers Memorial Fund. https://nleomf.org/slave-patrols-an-early-form-of-american-policing/

The 1619 Project. (2019, August 18). The New York Times Magazine. https://www.nytimes.com/interactive/2019/08/14/magazine/1619-america-slavery.html

#8 Anti-Literacy Laws in the United States (1740–1865)

Anele, U. (2020, February). *Anti-literacy Laws in the United States Once Prevented Blacks from Getting an Education.* Listwand. https://listwand.com/anti-literacy-laws-in-the-united-states-once-prevented-black-men-from-getting-an-education/

Banks, W. M. (1996). *Black Intellectuals: Race and Responsibility in American Life.* W. W. Norton & Company.

Cantu, A. (2016, September). *The Freedmen's Bureau and the Education of the Freedmen.* StMU Research Scholars. https://stmuhistorymedia.org/education-of-the-freedmens-bureau/

Cornelius, J. D. (1992). *When I Can Read My Title Clear: Literacy, Slavery, and Religion in the Antebellum South.* University of South Carolina Press.

Finkelman, P. (2006, April). *Encyclopedia of African American History, 1619–1895: From the Colonial Period to the Age of Frederick Douglass: (Encyclopedia of African American Culture and History), Volume 1, 2 & 3* (1st ed.). Oxford University Press, USA, p. 445.

History.com Editors (2018, October 3). *Freedmen's Bureau.* HISTORY. https://www.history.com/topics/black-history/freedmens-bureau

Illegal to Teach Slaves to Read and Write. (1862, June). Harper's Weekly. http://www.sonofthesouth.net/leefoundation/civil-war/1862/june/slaves-read-write.htm

Literacy and Anti-Literacy Laws. (n.d.). Encyclopedia.com. https://www.encyclopedia.com/humanities/applied-and-social-sciences-magazines/literacy-and-anti-literacy-laws

Shulman, J. (2018, August). *A right to literacy as the "Pathway from Slavery to Freedom"?.* National Constitution Center. https://constitutioncenter.org/blog/a-right-to-literacy-as-the-pathway-from-slavery-to-freedom

Span, C. M., & Sanya, B. N. (2019). Education and the African Diaspora. *The [Oxford] Handbook of the History of Education*, 398–412. https://doi.org/10.1093/oxfordhb/9780199340033.013.23

Stone-Palmquist, P. (2020, February). *Still Not Free: Connecting the Dots of Education Injustice*. Dignity in Schools. https://dignityinschools.org/still-not-free-connecting-the-dots-of-education-injustice/

The Freedmen's Bureau. (n.d.). Khan Academy. https://www.khanacademy.org/humanities/us-history/civil-war-era/reconstruction/a/the-freedmens-bureau

#9 Three-Fifths Compromise (1787)

Amdt14.S2.1.1 Apportionment Clause. (n.d.). Constitution Annotated | Congress.gov | Library of Congress. https://constitution.congress.gov/browse/essay/amdt14-S2-1-1/ALDE_00000847/

Conner, M. (2019, June 28). *Florida's Modern-Day Poll Tax*. Center for American Progress. https://americanprogress.org/article/floridas-modern-day-poll-tax/

DeRienzo, M. (2020, October 28). *Analysis: New and age-old voter suppression tactics at the heart of the 2020 power struggle*. The Center for Public Integrity. https://publicintegrity.org/politics/elections/ballotboxbarriers/analysis-voter-suppression-never-went-away-tactics-changed/

Friedman, W. (2006, January). *Fourteenth Amendment*. Encyclopedia of African-American Culture and History. HighBeam Research. https://web.archive.org/web/20140714223753/http:/www.highbeam.com/doc/1G2-3444700477.html

Madison, J. (1902).*The Writings, vol 3* (1787) . G. P. Putnam's Sons. Online Library of Liberty. https://oll.libertyfund.org/title/madison-the-writings-vol-3-1787

Nellis, A. (2021, October 13). *The Color of Justice: Racial and Ethnic Disparity in State Prisons*. The Sentencing Project. https://www.sentencingproject.org/publications/color-of-justice-racial-and-ethnic-disparity-in-state-prisons/

Poverty Rate by Race/Ethnicity. (2020, October 23). Kaiser Family Foundation. https://www.kff.org/other/state-indicator/poverty-rate-by-raceethnicity/?currentTimeframe=0&sortModel=%7B%22colId%22%3A%22Location%22%2C%22sort%22%3A%22asc%22%7D

The Constitution of the United States: A Transcription. National Archives and Records Administration.

U.S. Census Bureau QuickFacts: Florida. (n.d.). Census Bureau QuickFacts. https://www.census.gov/quickfacts/fact/table/FL/PST045219

#10 Fugitive Slave Acts (1793 & 1850)

Bowers, W. J., Sandys, M., & Brewer, T. W. (2004). Crossing Racial Boundaries: A Closer Look at the Roots of Racial Bias in Capital Sentencing When the Defendant is Black and the Victim is White. *DePaul Law Review*, 53(4), 1497–1538. https://via.library.depaul.edu/cgi/viewcontent.cgi?referer=&httpsredir=1&article=1476&context=law-review

Gates, H. L. (n.d.). *Free Blacks Lived in the North, Right?*. The African Americans: Many Rivers to Cross. PBS. Originally posted on The Root. https://www.pbs.org/wnet/african-americans-many-rivers-to-cross/history/free-blacks-lived-in-the-north-right/

Ghandnoosh, N. *(2015) Black Lives Matter: Eliminating Racial Inequity in the Criminal Justice System*. The Sentencing Project. https://sentencingproject.org/wp-content/uploads/2015/11/Black-Lives-Matter.pdf

History.com Editors (2020, February 12). *Fugitive Slave Acts.* HISTORY. https://www.history.com/topics/black-history/fugitive-slave-acts

O'Neill, A. (2021, March 19). *Black and slave population in the United States 1790-1880*. Statista. https://www.statista.com/statistics/1010169/black-and-slave-population-us-1790-1880/

Rapping, J. A. (2014, January 14). Implicitly Unjust: How Defenders Can Affect Systemic Racist Assumptions. *SSRN Electronic Journal. Published.* http://dx.doi.org/10.2139/ssrn.2380002

Sommers, S. R. (2006). On Racial Diversity and Group Decision Making: Identifying Multiple Effects of Racial Composition on Jury Deliberations. *Journal of Personality and Social Psychology*, 90(4), 597–612. https://doi.org/10.1037/0022-3514.90.4.597

The 1619 Project. (2019, August 18). The New York Times Magazine. https://www.nytimes.com/interactive/2019/08/14/magazine/1619-america-slavery.html

#11—Slavery's Deadly Commodities (Early 1800s)

The 1619 Project. (2019, August 18). The New York Times Magazine. https://www.nytimes.com/interactive/2019/08/14/magazine/1619-america-slavery.html

Wiegand, S. (2016, March 26). *Slavery Grows in 1800s America as Cotton and Sugar Production Increases*. Dummies.com. https://www.dummies.com/article/academics-the-arts/history/american/slavery-grows-in-1800s-america-as-cotton-and-sugar-production-increases-151534

#12 Medical Experiments on Black People

Baker, S. M., Brawley, O. W., & Marks, L. S. (2005, June). Effects of untreated syphilis in the negro male, 1932 to 1972: A closure comes to the Tuskegee study, 2004. *Urology*, 65(6), 1259–1262. https://doi.org/10.1016/j.urology.2004.10.023

DeGruy, J.A. (2017). *Post Traumatic Slave Syndrome: America's Legacy of Enduring Injury and Healing.* Joy DeGruy Publications Incorporated. pp. 61-63. ISBN 978-0985217273.

Duff-Brown, B. (2017, January 6). *The shameful legacy of Tuskegee syphilis study still impacts African-American men today.* Stanford Health Policy. https://healthpolicy.fsi.stanford.edu/news/researchers-and-students-run-pilot-project-oakland-test-whether-tuskegee-syphilis-trial-last

Excerpt: 'The Immortal Life of Henrietta Lacks' (2010, January 31). ABC News. https://abcnews.go.com/WN/immortal-life-henrietta-lacks-excerpt/story?id=9712490

Hoffman, K. M., Trawalter, S., Axt, J. R., & Oliver, M. N. (2016, April). Racial bias in pain assessment and treatment recommendations, and false beliefs about biological differences between blacks and whites. *Proceedings of the National Academy of Sciences, 113*(16), 4296–4301. https://doi.org/10.1073/pnas.1516047113

Holland, B. (2020, December 4). *The 'Father of Modern Gynecology' Performed Shocking Experiments on Enslaved Women.* HISTORY. https://www.history.com/news/the-father-of-modern-gynecology-performed-shocking-experiments-on-slaves

Khan, F. A. (2011, August 10). The Immortal Life of Henrietta Lacks. *Journal of the Islamic Medical Association of North America, 43*(2). https://doi.org/10.5915/43-2-8609

Kimble, L. (2017, February 16). *Henrietta Lacks' Family to Sue for Compensation for Her Medically Revolutionary Cells.* Yahoo Entertainment. https://www.yahoo.com/entertainment/henrietta-lacks-family-sue-compensation-205436402.html

Legha, R., Williams, D., Snowden, L. Miranda, J. (2020, November 4). *Getting Our Knees Off Black People's Necks: AN Anti-Racist Approach to Medical Care.* Health Affairs Blog. https://www.healthaffairs.org/do/10.1377/hblog20201029.167296/full/

Marcus, A. D. (2020, August 1). *Henrietta Lacks and Her Remarkable Cells Will Finally See Some Payback.* The Wall Street Journal. https://www.wsj.com/articles/henrietta-lacks-and-her-remarkable-cells-will-finally-see-some-payback-11596295285

Newkirk, V. R. II (2016, June 17). *A Generation of Bad Blood.* The Atlantic. https://www.theatlantic.com/politics/archive/2016/06/tuskegee-study-medical-distrust-research/487439/

O'Neal, L. (2020) *Half of Black adults say they won't take a coronavirus vaccine.* The Undefeated. https://theundefeated.com/features/half-of-Black-adults-say-they-wont-take-a-coronavirus-vaccine/

Racism and Health. (2021, November 24). Centers for Disease Control and Prevention. https://www.cdc.gov/healthequity/racism-disparities/index.html

Racism is a Public Health Crisis. (n.d.). American Public Health Association. https://www.apha.org/topics-and-issues/health-equity/racism-and-health/racism-declarations

Stern, A.M. (2020, August 29). *A History of Forced Sterilization in the United States.* The National Interest. https://nationalinterest.org/blog/reboot/history-forced-sterilization-united-states-167762

Tafesse, K. (2019, May 1). *What the 'Mississippi Appendectomy' says about the regard of the state towards the agency of black women's bodies.* The Movement for Black Women's Lives. https://blackwomenintheblackfreedomstruggle.voices.wooster.edu/2019/05/01/what-the-mississippi-appendectomy-says-about-the-regard-of-the-state-towards-the-agency-of-black-womens-bodies/

U.S. Public Health Service Syphilis Study at Tuskegee. The Tuskegee Timeline. *(n.d.).* United States Centers for Disease Control and Prevention. https://www.cdc.gov/tuskegee/timeline.htm

Yecheilyah (2020, July 24). *Black History Fun Fact Friday—"Drapetomania."* The PBS Blog. https://thepbsblog.com/2020/07/24/black-history-fun-fact-friday-drapetomania/

#13 Justify Racism through Mental Illness

APA apologizes for longstanding contributions to systemic racism. (2021, October 29). American Psychological Association. https://www.apa.org/news/press/releases/2021/10/apology-systemic-racism

Brown, A. (2020, October 13). *What is PTSS? Post-Traumatic Syndrome Explained.* The Moguldom Nation. https://moguldom.com/310304/what-is-ptss-post-traumatic-slave-syndrome-explained/#:~:text=But%20post-traumatic%20slave%20syndrome%20also%20differs%20from%20post-traumatic,as%20individuals%20facing%20constant%20stress%20from%20everyday%20racism

Caplan, A.L., McCartney, J.J., & Sisti, D.A., & Md, E.P.D. (2004). *Health, Disease, and Illness: concepts in medicine* (1st ed.). Georgetown University Press. ISBN 1589010140.

DeGruy, J.A. (2017). *Post Traumatic Slave Syndrome: America's Legacy of Enduring Injury and Healing* (Revised ed.). Joy DeGruy Publications Incorporated. ISBN 978-0985217273.

Dimuro, G. (2018, April 4). *Southerners Actually Thought Slaves Escaping Was a Sign of Mental Illness.* All That's Interesting. https://allthatsinteresting.com/drapetomania

Legha, R.K., Williams, D.R., Snowden, L. & Miranda, J. (2020, November 4). *Getting Our Knees Off of Black People's Necks: An Anti-Racist Approach to Care.* HealthAffairs. org. https://www.healthaffairs.org/do/10.1377/hblog20201029.167296/full/

Racism and Health. (2021, November 24). Centers for Disease Control and Prevention. https://www.cdc.gov/healthequity/racism-disparities/index.html

Racism is a Public Health Crisis. (n.d.). American Public Health Association. https://www.apha.org/topics-and-issues/health-equity/racism-and-health/racism-declarations

Talk Africana. (2021, June 25). *Drapetomania: Enslave Africans Fleeing Captivity Was Once Considered a Mental Disorder.* Listwand. https://listwand.com/drapetomania-fleeing-from-a-master-was-once-considered-a-mental-disorder/

White, K. (2002). *An introduction to the Sociology of Health and Illness.* SAGE Publications Ltd. pp. 41, 42. ISBN 0761964002.

Yecheilyah (2020, July 24). *Black History Fun Fact Friday—"Drapetomania."* The PBS Blog. https://thepbsblog.com/2020/07/24/black-history-fun-fact-friday-drapetomania/

#14 *Dred Scott v. Sandford* (1857)

Biography.com Editors (2021, May 12). *Dred Scott Biography.* Biography.com. https://www.biography.com/activist/dred-scott

Chemerinsky, E. (2015). *The Case Against the Supreme Court (Reprint ed.).* Penguin Books.

Ehrlich, W. (1968, September). Was the Dred Scott Case Valid? *The Journal of American History,* 55 (2): 256-265. https://doi.org/10.2307/1899556

Enslaved African Americans and the Fight for Freedom. (n.d.). Minnesota Historical Society. https://www.mnhs.org/fortsnelling/learn/african-americans

Fehrenbacher, D.E. (2001). *The Dred Scott Case: Its Significance in American Law and Politics (First Paperback ed.).* Oxford University Press.

Hardy, D. T. (2012, December 2). *Dred Scott, John San(d)ford, and the Case for Collusion.* Northern Kentucky Law Review. 41 (1). http://dx.doi.org/10.2139/ssrn.2183939

Mintz, S. (2007). *The Problem of Evil: Slavery, Freedom and the Ambiguities of American Reform* (Illustrated ed.). University of Massachusetts Press.

Missouri's Dred Scott Case, 1846-1857 (n.d.). Missouri State Archives. https://www.sos.mo.gov/archives/resources/africanamerican/scott/scott.asp

Nowak, J., & Rotunda, R. (2009). *Constitutional Law (Hornbooks)* (8th ed.). West Academic Publishing. ISBN: 978-0314195999.

#15 Emancipation Proclamation (1863)

Abraham Lincoln's Emancipation Proclamation. (n.d.). American Battlefield Trust. https://www.battlefields.org/learn/primary-sources/abraham-lincolns-emancipation-proclamation

Civil War Facts. (n.d.). National Park Service. https://www.nps.gov/civilwar/facts.htm

History.com Editors. (2021, January 13). *Civil War.* HISTORY. https://www.history.com/topics/american-civil-war/american-civil-war-history

O'Neill, A. (2021, March 19). *Black and slave population in the United States 1790-1880.* Statista. https://www.statista.com/statistics/1010169/black-and-slave-population-us-1790-1880/

The Emancipation Proclamation. (n.d.). Khan Academy. https://www.khanacademy.org/humanities/us-history/civil-war-era/slavery-and-the-civil-war/a/the-emancipation-proclamation

The Emancipation Proclamation. (2021, August 5). National Archives. https://www.archives.gov/exhibits/featured-documents/emancipation-proclamation

#16 Civil War (1861–1865)

Abraham Lincoln's Emancipation Proclamation. (n.d.) American Battlefield Trust. https://www.battlefields.org/learn/primary-sources/abraham-lincolns-emancipation-proclamation

Civil War Facts. (n.d.). National Park Service. https://www.nps.gov/civilwar/facts.htm

History.com Editors. (2021, January 13). *Civil War.* HISTORY. https://www.history.com/topics/american-civil-war/american-civil-war-history

O'Neill, A. (2021, March 19). *Black and slave population in the United States 1790-1880.* Statista. https://www.statista.com/statistics/1010169/black-and-slave-population-us-1790-1880/

The Emancipation Proclamation (n.d.). Khan Academy. https://www.khanacademy. org/humanities/us-history/civil-war-era/slavery-and-the-civil-war/a/ the-emancipation-proclamation

The Emancipation Proclamation. (2021, August 5). National Archives. https://www.archives.gov/exhibits/featured-documents/emancipation-proclamation

U.S. Civil War Took Bigger Toll Than Previously Estimated, New Analysis Suggests. (2011, September). Science Daily. https://www.sciencedaily.com/ releases/2011/09/110921120124.htm

#17 Juneteenth (1865)

Adams, L. (2010). *Way Up North in Louisville: African American Migration in the Urban South, 1930–1970 (The John Hope Franklin Series in African American History and Culture).* University of North Carolina Press. ISBN 978-0807899434.

Campbell, R.B. (1984). The End of Slavery in Texas: A Research Note. *The Southwestern Historical Quarterly.* 88 (1), 71–80. http://www.jstor.org/stable/30239840

Garrett-Scott, S., Richardson, R. C., & Dillard-Allen, V. (2013). "When Peace Come": Teaching the Significance of Juneteenth. *Black History Bulletin,* 76(2), 19–25. http://www.jstor.org/stable/24759690

Gates, H. L. (n.d.). *What Is Juneteenth?.* The African Americans: Many Rivers to Cross. PBS. Originally posted on The Root. https://www.pbs.org/wnet/ african-americans-many-rivers-to-cross/history/what-is-juneteenth/

Harlem World Magazine (2020, June). *Juneteenth, The 155th Year Of American History From Harlem To Harare (Video).* https://www.harlemworldmagazine.com/ juneteenth-the-155th-year-of-american-history-from-harlem-to- harare-video/

It Happened: June 19. (1974, June). Milwaukee Star, 14(42).

Juneteenth Adds Continuity to Black Tradition. Fort Worth Star-Telegram. p. 100. Retrieved June 4, 2020—via Newspapers.com

Juneteenth. Texas State Library and Archives Commission.

Knight, G. (2011). Juneteenth. *Encyclopedia of African American Popular Culture.* Greenwood. pp. 798–801. OCLC 694734649.

Smith, J.C. & Wynn, L. T. (2009). *Freedom Facts and Firsts: 400 Years of the African American Civil Rights Experience.* Amsterdam University Press.

#18 Thirteenth Amendment (1865)

Alexander, M. (2010, January). *The New Jim Crow: Mass Incarceration in the Age of Colorblindness.* The New Press.

America's Opportunity Gaps: By the Numbers. (2020, June). U.S. Chamber of Commerce. https://www.uschamber.com/workforce/education/us-chamber- releases-america-s-opportunity-gaps-the-numbers-examining-underlying

Convict Leasing. (2013, November 1). Equal Justice Initiative. https://eji.org/news/ history-racial-injustice-convict-leasing/

Forbes, F. (2019, June 3). *How a 13th Amendment Loophole Created America's Carceral State*. The Crime Report. https://thecrimereport.org/2019/06/03/539754/

From Slavery to Mass Incarceration. (2019, August 23). Ben & Jerry's. https://www.benjerry.com/whats-new/2019/08/slavery-to-mass-incarceration

Garcia, C. (2020, June). *The Uncounted Workforce*. NPR. https://www.npr.org/transcripts/884989263

History.com Editors. (2020, June 19). *13th Amendment*. HISTORY. https://www.history.com/topics/black-history/thirteenth-amendment

Mesa, C. (2020, June 19). *Yes, The Thirteenth Amendment Really Does Have a Loophole That Allows Slavery—Just Look at our Prison System*. MITU. https://wearemitu.com/entertainment/yes-the-thirteenth-amendment-really-does-have-a-loophole-that-allows-slavery-just-look-at-our-prison-system/

Mulvaney, K. (2014, December 7). *PolitiFact—Brown U. student leader: More African-American men in prison system now than were enslaved in 1850*. (2014) Politifact. https://www.politifact.com/factchecks/2014/dec/07/diego-arene-morley/brown-u-student-leader-more-african-american-men-p/

#19 Reconstruction (1865–1877)

A 1905 Silent Movie Revolutionizes American Film—and Radicalizes American Nationalists. (2018, January). Southern Hollows Podcast. http://www.southernhollows.com/episodes/birthofanation

Baker, B.E. (2007). *What Reconstruction Meant: Historical Memory in the American South*. University of Virginia Press. ISBN 978-0813926605.

Foner, E. (2021, November 5). *Reconstruction-United States History*. Encyclopedia Britannica. https://www.britannica.com/event/Reconstruction-United-States-history

Gates, H.L. (2019, April). *How Reconstruction Still Shapes American Racism*. Time. https://time.com/5562869/reconstruction-history/

Landmark Legislation: Thirteenth, Fourteenth, & Fifteenth Amendments. (n.d.). United States Senate. https://www.senate.gov/artandhistory/history/common/generic/CivilWarAmendments.htm

Lemann, N. (2006). *Redemption: The Last Battle of the Civil War* (1st ed.). Farrar, Straus and Giroux. pp. 75–77. ISBN 978-0374248550.

McPherson, J.M. (1992). *Abraham Lincoln and the Second American Revolution*. Oxford University Press. p. 19. ISBN 978-0195076066.

The Battle Over Reconstruction. (n.d.). Lumen Learning. https://courses.lumenlearning.com/boundless-ushistory/chapter/the-battle-over-reconstruction/#:~:text=In%20March%201865%2C%20Congress%20created,new%20agency%2C%20the%20Freedmen's%20Bureau.&text=With%20the%20help%20of%20the,of%20labor%20in%20many%20areas.

#20 Forty Acres and a Mule (1865)

Foner, E. (2021, November 5). *Reconstruction*. Encyclopedia Britannica. https://www.britannica.com/event/Reconstruction-United-States-history

Forty acres and a mule: after the Civil War, 4 million former slaves had their freedom—but not much else. What could be done to help get them on their feet?. (2014). The Free Library. (2014). https://www.thefreelibrary.com/Forty +acres+and+a+mule%3a+after+the+Civil+War%2c+4+million+former+ slaves...-a0129368292

Gates, H.L. (2013, January 7). *The Truth Behind '40 Acres and a Mule'*. The Root. https://www.theroot.com/the-truth-behind-40-acres- and-a-mule-1790894780

History.com Editors. (2021, January 21). *Reconstruction*. HISTORY. https://www.history.com/topics/american-civil-war/reconstruction

McCurdy, D. (2007, December 15). *Forty Acres and a Mule*. Black Past. https://www.Blackpast.org/african-american-history/forty-acres-and-mule/

Understanding and Dismantling Systemic Racism in Housing. (n.d.). Divvy Blog. https://blog.divvyhomes.com/2020/06/30/systemic-racism-in-housing/

#21 Ku Klux Klan

A 1905 Silent Movie Revolutionizes American Film—and Radicalizes American Nationalists. (2018, January). Southern Hollows Podcast. http://www. southernhollows.com/episodes/birthofanation

Clark, A. (2019, July 29). *How 'The Birth of a Nation' Revived the Ku Klux Klan*. HISTORY. https://www.history.com/news/kkk-birth-of-a-nation-film

Gates, H.L. (2019, April). *How Reconstruction Still Shapes American Racism*. Time. https://time.com/5562869/reconstruction-history/

Knickerbocker, Brad (2007, February 9). *Anti-immigrant sentiments fuel Ku Klux Klan resurgence*. The Christian Science Monitor. https://www.csmonitor.com/2007/0209/ p02s02-ussc.html

Linder, Douglas O. *The Mississippi Burning Trial (U. S. vs. Price et al.)*. (n.d.). Famous Trials. University of Missouri-Kansas City School of Law. https://web.archive.org/web/20081014003534/http://www.law.umkc.edu/faculty/ projects/ftrials/price%26bowers/Account.html

Lynn, S., & Thorbecke, C. (2020, September 27). *What America owes: How reparations would look and who would pay*. ABC News. https://abcnews.go.com/Business/ america-owes-reparations-pay/story?id=72863094

Martinez, J.M. (2007). *Carpetbaggers, Cavalry, and the Ku Klux Klan: Exposing the Invisible Empire During Reconstruction (The American Crisis Series: Books on the Civil War Era)*. Rowman & Littlefield Publishers. p. 24. ISBN 978-0742572614.

Pilgrim, D. (2012). *What was Jim Crow*. Ferris State University-Jim Crow Museum of Racist Memorabilia. https://www.ferris.edu/jimcrow/what.htm

Protecting Life and Property: Passing the Ku Klux Klan Act (U.S. National Park Service). (n.d.). National Park Service. https://www.nps.gov/articles/000/protecting-life-and-property-passing-the-ku-klux-klan-act.htm

Trelease, A.W. (1979). *White Terror: The Ku Klux Klan Conspiracy and Southern Reconstruction.* Praeger. ISBN: 978-0313211683.

#22 Lost Cause Ideology

Blight, D.W. (2001). *Race and Reunion: The Civil War in American Memory.* Belknap/Harvard University Press. p. 259. ISBN 978-0674003323.

Blight, D.W. (2021, September 20). *Lost Cause. Encyclopedia Britannica.* https://www.britannica.com/topic/Lost-Cause

Confederate Symbols Are Making Way for Better Things. (2021, February). Associated Press. https://enewspaper.latimes.com/infinity/article_share.aspx?guid=bfb284f1-9b32-4419-ad7b-205953ac2c73

Cox, K. L. (2019). *Dixie's Daughters: The United Daughters of the Confederacy and the Preservation of Confederate Culture.* University Press of Florida. ISBN 978-0813064130.

Domby, A.H. (2020, February). *The False Cause: Fraud, Fabrication, and White Supremacy in Confederate Memory.* University of Virginia Press. ISBN 978-0-813943763. OCLC 1151896244.

Foster, G.M. (1988), *Ghosts of the Confederacy: Defeat, the Lost Cause and the Emergence of the New South, 1865–1913.* Oxford University Press. ISBN: 978-0195054200.

Gallagher, G.W. & Nolan, A.T. (2000). *The Myth of the Lost Cause and Civil War History.* Indiana University Press. ISBN 978-0253338228.

Jones, R.P. (2020, July 28). *Racism among white Christians is higher than among the nonreligious. That's no coincidence.* Think-NBC News. https://www.nbcnews.com/think/opinion/racism-among-white-christians-higher-among-nonreligious-s-no-coincidence-ncna1235045

#23 The Compromise of 1877

APUSH Study Notes. (n.d.). Quizlet. https://quizlet.com/32207996/apush-study-notes-flash-cards/

Benedict, M.L. (1980) Southern Democrats in the Crisis of 1876-1877: A Reconstruction of Reunion and Reaction. *Journal of Southern History, 46(4)* 489-524. https://doi.org/10.2307/2207200

Compromise of 1877. (2018, January 31). Quizlet. https://quizlet.com/266792838/compromise-of-1877-1312018-flash-cards/

Deskins, D.R., Walton, H., & Puckett, S.C. (2010). *Presidential Elections, 1789-2008: County, State, and National Mapping of Election Data.* University of Michigan Press. p. 211. ISBN 978-0472026777.

History.om Editors. (2019, November 27). *Compromise of 1877*. HISTORY. https://www.history.com/topics/us-presidents/compromise-of-1877

Woodward, C.V. (1991). *Reunion and Reaction: The Compromise of 1877 and the End of Reconstruction*. Oxford University Press. pp. 200–202. ISBN 978-0195064230.

#24 Jim Crow (1877–1968)

A Brief History of Civil Rights in the United States.(2021, August) Georgetown Law Library. https://guides.ll.georgetown.edu/c.php?g=592919&p=4100954

Pilgrim, D. (2012). *What was Jim Crow*. Ferris State University-Jim Crow Museum of Racist Memorabilia. https://www.ferris.edu/jimcrow/what.htm

Shvili, J. (2021, November 8). *The Black Code And Jim Crow Laws*. WorldAtlas. https://www.worldatlas.com/articles/who-was-jim-crow-and-what-was-his-purpose.html

Sims, M. (n.d.). *Separate not Equal: Plessy v. Ferguson's Influence on Modern Discrimination*. The Making of the Modern U.S. http://projects.leadr.msu.edu/makingmodernus/exhibits/show/plessy-v--ferguson-1896

Understanding and Dismantling Systemic Racism in Housing. (n.d.). Divvy Blog. https://blog.divvyhomes.com/2020/06/30/systemic-racism-in-housing/

#25 Sharecropping (1860s–1950s)

A Brief History of Civil Rights in the United States.(2021, August) Georgetown Law Library. https://guides.ll.georgetown.edu/c.php?g=592919&p=4100954

History.com Editors (2019, June 7). *Sharecropping*. HISTORY. https://www.history.com/topics/black-history/sharecropping

Jaynes, G.D. (2020, August 27). *debt slavery*. Encyclopedia Britannica. https://www.britannica.com/topic/debt-slavery

O'Donovan, S.E. (2010). *Becoming Free in the Cotton South*. Harvard University Press. ISBN 978-0674041608.

Ransom, R.L. & Sutch, R. (2001). *One Kind of Freedom: The Economic Consequences of Emancipation* (2nd ed.). Cambridge University Press. ISBN 978-0521795500.

Rothstein, R. (2017, May). *The Color of Law: A Forgotten History of How Our Government Segregated America*. Liveright. ISBN 978-1631492853.

Sharecropping in the United States. (n.d.). Hinds Community College. https://hindscc.instructure.com/courses/176660/pages/sharecropping-in-the-united-states

Sharecropping. Slavery by Another Name. PBS. (n.d.). https://www.pbs.org/tpt/slavery-by-another-name/themes/sharecropping/

Sharecropping: The South's Attempt to Re-Establish the Labor System of Slavery. (2020, December). Black Then. https://blackthen.com/sharecropping-the-souths-attempt-to-re-establish-the-labor-system-of-slavery/

Understanding and Dismantling Systemic Racism in Housing. (n.d.). Divvy Blog. https://blog.divvyhomes.com/2020/06/30/systemic-racism-in-housing/

Wilkerson, I. (2016, September). *The Long-Lasting Legacy of the Great Migration.* Smithsonian Magazine. https://www.smithsonianmag.com/history/long-lasting-legacy-great-migration-180960118/

Wright, G. (1997). *Old South, New South: Revolutions in the Southern Economy Since the Civil War.* LSU Press. ISBN 978-0807120989.

#26 Lynchings/Massacres (Most Common 1880s–1960s)

Lartey, J. & Morris, S. (2018, April). *How white Americans used lynchings to terrorize and control black people.* The Guardian. https://www.theguardian.com/us-news/2018/apr/26/lynchings-memorial-us-south-montgomery-alabama

Myrdal, G. (1944). *An American Dilemma: The Negro Problem and Modern Democracy.* Harper & Bros. p. 561. ISBN 978-1560008569.

NAACP. (2021, May 9). *History of Lynching in America.* https://naacp.org/find-resources/history-explained/history-lynching-america

Pilgrim, D. (2012). *What was Jim Crow.* Ferris State University-Jim Crow Museum of Racist Memorabilia. https://www.ferris.edu/jimcrow/what.htm

#27 NAACP (1909–Present)

Appiah, K. A., & Gates, H. L. (2003). *Africana: The Encyclopedia of the African and African American Experience—The Concise Desk Reference* (1st Edition). Running Press. ISBN 0762416424.

Britannica, T. Editors of Encyclopaedia (2019, November 5). *National Association for the Advancement of Colored People.* Encyclopedia Britannica. https://www.britannica.com/topic/National-Association-for-the-Advancement-of-Colored-People

History.com Editors. (2021, January 25). *NAACP.* HISTORY. https://www.history.com/topics/civil-rights-movement/naacp

History.com Editors. (2021, April 27). Black History Milestones: Timeline. HISTORY. https://www.history.com/topics/black-history/black-history-milestones

NAACP *(2021, May 11). Our History.* https://naacp.org/about/our-history

NAACP (2008, June 11). *Our Mission.* https://web.archive.org/web/20080611053922/http://www.naacp.org/about/mission/

Simkin, J. (2014, January). William English Walling Biography. Spartacus Educational. https://spartacus-educational.com/USAwalling.htm

#28 Great Migration (1916–1970)

African Americans—The age of Booker T. Washington. (n.d.). Encyclopedia Britannica. https://www.britannica.com/topic/African-American/The-age-of-Booker-T-Washington

Great Migration | Definition, History, & Facts. (n.d.). Encyclopedia Britannica. https://www.britannica.com/event/Great-Migration

Hine, D., Hine, W. & Harrold, S. (2012). *African Americans: A Concise History* (4th ed.). Boston: Pearson Education, Inc. pp. 388–389. ISBN 978-0205806270.

History.com Editors. (2021, June 28). *The Great Migration.* HISTORY. https://www.history.com/topics/black-history/great-migration

Kopf, D. (2016, January). *The Great Migration: The African American Exodus from The South.* Priceonomics. https://priceonomics.com/the-great-migration-the-african-american-exodus/

Lynchings: By State and Race, 1882–1968. (n.d.). University of Missouri-Kansas City School of Law. http://law2.umkc.edu/faculty/projects/ftrials/shipp/lynchingsstate.html

The Great Migration (n.d.). Smithsonian American Art Museum. https://americanexperience.si.edu/wp-content/uploads/2014/07/The-Great-Migration.pdf

Wilkerson, I. (2011). *The Warmth of Other Suns: The Epic Story of America's Great Migration* (Reprint ed.). Vintage. ISBN 978-0679763888.

Wilkerson, I. (2016, September). *The Long-Lasting Legacy of the Great Migration. Smithsonian Magazine.* https://www.smithsonianmag.com/history/long-lasting-legacy-great-migration-180960118/

#29 The Green Book (1936–1967)

Andrews, E. (2019, March 13). *The Green Book: The Black Travelers' Guide to Jim Crow America.* HISTORY. https://www.history.com/news/the-green-book-the-black-travelers-guide-to-jim-crow-america

Franz, K., & Smulyan, S. (2011). *Major Problems in American Popular Culture (Major Problems in American History Series)* (001 ed.). Cengage Learning. ISBN 978-1133417170.

Giorgis, H. (2019, February 25). *The Documentary Highlighting the Real Green Book.* The Atlantic. https://www.theatlantic.com/entertainment/archive/2019/02/real-green-book-preserving-stories-of-jim-crow-era-travel/583294/

Goodavage, M. (2013, January). *'Green Book' Helped Keep African Americans Safe on the Road.* PBS. https://www.pbs.org/independentlens/blog/green-book-helped-keep-african-americans-safe-on-the-road/

Seiler, C. (2006). *"So That We as a Race Might Have Something Authentic to Travel By": African American Automobility and Cold-War Liberalism.* American Quarterly, 58(4), 1091–1117. http://www.jstor.org/stable/40068407

Slethaug, G.E. & Ford, S. (2017). *Hit the Road, Jack: Essays on the Culture of the American Road.* McGill-Queen's University Press. ISBN 978-0773540767.

#30 GI Bill (1944–1956)

Altschuler, G. & Blumin, S. (2009) *The GI Bill: A New Deal for Veterans (Pivotal Moments in American History).* New York: Oxford University Press. p. 118. ISBN 978-0195182286.

Baker, P.C. (2016, November 27). *The Tragic, Forgotten History of Black Military Veterans*. The New Yorker. https://www.newyorker.com/news/news-desk/the-tragic-forgotten-history-of-black-military-veterans

Blakemore, E. (2021, April 20). *How the GI Bill's Promise Was Denied to a Million Black WWII Veterans*. History.com. https://www.history.com/news/gi-bill-black-wwii-veterans-benefits

Brooker, R. (n.d.). *The Education of Black Children in the Jim Crow South*. America's Black Holocaust Museum. https://www.abhmuseum.org/education-for-blacks-in-the-jim-crow-south/

Dailey, B.J. (2005, November 27). *Some unexpected links in the chain of American racial inequality*. The Chicago Tribune. https://www.chicagotribune.com/news/ct-xpm-2005-11-27-0511260109-story.html

Darity, W.A., & Mullen, A.K. (2020). *From Here to Equality: Reparations for Black Americans in the Twenty-First century*. University of North Carolina Press. ISBN 978-1469654973.

Herbold, H. (1994). Never a Level Playing Field: Blacks and the GI Bill. *The Journal of Blacks in Higher Education, 6*, 104–108. https://doi.org/10.2307/2962479.

Katznelson, I. (2005). *When Affirmative Action Was White: An Untold History of Racial Inequality in Twentieth-century America*. W. W. Norton & Co. p. 140. ISBN 978-0393328516.

Kotz, N. (2005, August 28). *"When Affirmative Action Was White": Uncivil Rights*. The New York Times. https://www.nytimes.com/2005/08/28/books/review/when-affirmative-action-was-white-uncivil-rights.html?_r=0

Morrison, A., & Stafford, K. (2021, November 11). *Black WWII veterans were denied GI Bill benefits. Veterans Day legislation looks to correct that now*. Chicagotribune.Com. https://www.chicagotribune.com/nation-world/ct-aud-nw-gi-bill-racial-inequities-20211111-fbihr7f73nefdi3iav7q2nkoq4-story.html

Szapiro, Aron (2020, October 6). *Can Baby Bonds Shrink the Racial Wealth Gap?* Morningstar, Inc. https://www.morningstar.com/articles/1003066/can-baby-bonds-shrink-the-racial-wealth-gap

US Census Bureau. (2019, September). *Income and Poverty in the United States: 2018*. Census.Gov. https://www.census.gov/library/publications/2019/demo/p60-266.html

#31 Homeownership Injustices

America's Opportunity Gaps: By the Numbers. (2020, June). U.S. Chamber of Commerce. https://www.uschamber.com/workforce/education/us-chamber-releases-america-s-opportunity-gaps-the-numbers-examining-underlying

Dedman, B. (1988, May). *The Color of Money*. The Atlanta Journal-Constitution.

From Slavery to Mass Incarceration. (2019, August 23). Ben & Jerry's. https://www.benjerry.com/whats-new/2019/08/slavery-to-mass-incarceration

Jackson, K.T. (1985). *Crabgrass Frontier: The Suburbanization of the United States*. Oxford University Press. ISBN 0195049837.

Kahlenberg, R. (2017). *Why Segregated Neighborhoods Persist.* Washington Monthly. https://washingtonmonthly.com/magazine/junejulyaugust-2017/why-segregated-neighborhoods-persist/

Madrigal, A.C. (2014, May). *The Racist Housing Policy That Made Your Neighborhood.* The Atlantic. https://www.theatlantic.com/business/archive/2014/05/the-racist-housing-policy-that-made-your-neighborhood/371439/

Perry, A., & Harshbarger, D. (2019, October 14). *America's formerly redlined neighborhoods have changed, and so must solutions to rectify them.* The Brookings Institution. https://www.brookings.edu/research/americas-formerly-redlines-areas-changed-so-must-solutions/

Rothstein, R. (2017, May). *The Color of Law: A Forgotten History of How Our Government Segregated America.* Liveright. ISBN 978-1631492853.

Taylor, K.Y. (2018). *How Real Estate Segregated America.* Dissent Magazine. https://www.dissentmagazine.org/article/how-real-estate-segregated-america-fair-housing-act-race

The Plunder of Black Wealth in Chicago: New Findings on the Lasting Toll of Predatory Housing Contracts. (2019, May). The Samuel DuBois Cook Center on Social Equity at Duke University. https://socialequity.duke.edu/wp-content/uploads/2019/10/Plunder-of-Black-Wealth-in-Chicago.pdf

Understanding and Dismantling Systemic Racism in Housing. (n.d.). Divvy Blog. https://blog.divvyhomes.com/2020/06/30/systemic-racism-in-housing/

Wilson, W.J. (1997). *When Work Disappears: The World of the New Urban Poor.* Vintage. ISBN 0679724176.

#32 American Federalism (States' Rights vs. Federal Authority)

African American Studies: Study Guide. (n.d.). Quizlet. https://quizlet.com/136085866/african-american-studies-study-guide-flash-cards/

Barnett, R.E., & Gerken, K. (n.d.). *Article I, Sec. 8: Federalism and the Overall Scope of Federal Power | The National Constitution Center.* (n.d.). Constitution Center. https://constitutioncenter.org/interactive-constitution/interpretation/article-i/section/8712

Civil Rights Movement. (n.d.). Anti-Defamation League. https://www.adl.org/education/resources/backgrounders/civil-rights-movement

Constitution of the United States. *United States Senate.* https://www.senate.gov/civics/constitution_item/constitution.htm#a4

Cox, C. (2020, June 14). *Fact check: National Guard was activated most often during the Civil Rights Era.* USA TODAY. https://eu.usatoday.com/story/news/factcheck/2020/06/14/fact-check-national-guard-activated-16-times-us/5319853002/

History.com Editors. (2021, January 13). *Civil War.* HISTORY. https://www.history.com/topics/american-civil-war/american-civil-war-history

Longley, R. (2019). *Federalism and How It Works*. ThoughtCo. https://www.thoughtco.com/what-is-federalism-3321880

Roos, D. (2020, April). *When the Founding Fathers Settled States' vs. Federal Rights—And Saved the Nation*. HISTORY. https://www.history.com/news/federalism-constitution-founding-fathers-states-rights

Shvili, J. (2021, November 8). *The Black Code And Jim Crow Laws*. WorldAtlas. https://www.worldatlas.com/articles/who-was-jim-crow-and-what-was-his-purpose.html

States' Rights. (n.d.) American Battlefield Trust. https://www.battlefields.org/learn/articles/states-rights

The relationship between the states and the federal government. (n.d.). Khan Academy. https://www.khanacademy.org/humanities/us-government-and-civics/us-gov-foundations/us-gov-relationship-between-the-states-and-the-federal-government/a/relationship-between-the-states-and-the-federal-government-article

The Supremacy Clause and Federal Preemption. (n.d.). Exploring Constitutional Conflicts. http://law2.umkc.edu/faculty/projects/ftrials/conlaw/preemption.htm

#33 Civil Rights Movement (1954–1968)

A Brief History of Civil Rights in the United States. (2021, August 26) Georgetown Law Library. https://guides.ll.georgetown.edu/c.php?g=592919&p=4100954

Civil Rights Act of 1968. (2013, March 7). U.S. Government Publishing Office. https://www.govinfo.gov/content/pkg/COMPS-343/pdf/COMPS-343.pdf

Civil Rights Division. (n.d.). Department of Justice. https://www.justice.gov/crt

Civil Rights Movement. (n.d.). Anti-Defamation League. https://www.adl.org/education/resources/backgrounders/civil-rights-movement

History of Fair Housing. (n.d.). United States Department of Housing and Urban Development. https://www.hud.gov/program_offices/fair_housing_equal_opp/aboutfheo/history

History of Federal Voting Rights Laws: The Voting Rights Act of 1965. (2017, July 28). United States Department of Justice. https://www.justice.gov/crt/history-federal-voting-rights-laws

History.com Editors. (2021, May 17). *Civil Rights Movement*. HISTORY. https://www.history.com/topics/black-history/civil-rights-movement

Introduction to Federal Voting Rights Laws: The Effect of the Voting Rights Act. (2009, June 19) U.S. Department of Justice. https://archive.md/aDLPt

Koussecr, J.M. (1974). *The Shaping of Southern Politics: Suffrage Restriction and the Establishment of the One-Party South, 1880-1910*. Yale University Press. ISBN 978-0300016963.

Lewis, J., & Allen, A.E. (1972, October 1). *Black Voter Registration Efforts in the South*. Notre Dame. https://scholarship.law.nd.edu/cgi/viewcontent.cgi?article=2861&context=ndlr

Parks Recalls Bus Boycott, Excerpts from an interview with Lynn Neary, National Public Radio, 1992, Linked at Civil Rights Icon Rosa Parks Dies. (2005, October25). NPR. https://www.npr.org/templates/story/story.php?storyId=4973548

Perman, M. (2001). *Struggle for Mastery: Disfranchisement in the South, 1888–1908.* University of North Carolina Press. ISBN 978-0807825938.

Shvili, J. (2021, November 8). *The Black Code And Jim Crow Laws.* WorldAtlas. https://www.worldatlas.com/articles/who-was-jim-crow-and-what-was-his-purpose.html

Stephens, O. & Scheb, J. (2007*). American Constitutional Law, Volume II: Civil Rights and Liberties* (4th ed.). Cengage Learning. p. 528. ISBN 978-0495097051.

Understanding and Dismantling Systemic Racism in Housing. (n.d.). Divvy Blog. https://blog.divvyhomes.com/2020/06/30/systemic-racism-in-housing/

Voting Rights Act. (n.d.). National Voting Rights Museum and Institute. http://nvrmi.com/?page_id=41

White, I.K. & Laird, C.N. (2020, February 25). *Why are Blacks Democrats?* Princeton. https://press.princeton.edu/ideas/why-are-blacks-democrats

#34 COINTELPRO (1956–1971)

Berberoglu, B. (2010). *Globalization in the 21st Century: Labor, Capital, and the State on a World Scale.* Palgrave MacMillan. ISBN 978-0230106390.

Bezanson, K., & Webber, M. (2016). *Rethinking Society in the 21st Century*, (4th ed.). Canadian Scholars. p. 148. ISBN 978-1551309361.

Branch, Taylor *(2007). Pillar of Fire: America in the King Years 1963–1965.* Simon & Schuster. pp. 524–529. ISBN 978-1416558705.

Cassidy, M., & Miller, W. (1999, May 26). *A Short History of FBI COINTELPRO.* Albion Monitor. https://web.archive.org/web/20070928104133/http:/www.albionmonitor.net/9905a/jbcointelpro.html

Churchill, W., & Vander Wall, J. (2002). *The COINTELPRO Papers: Documents from the FBI's Secret Wars Against Dissent in the United States.* South End Press. ISBN 978-0896086487.

Final Report of the Select Committee to Study Governmental Operations with Respect to Intelligence Activities, Book III: Supplementary Detailed Staff Reports on Intelligence Activities and the Rights of Americans (Final Report). (1976, April). United States Senate Report No. 94-755. https://www.intelligence.senate.gov/sites/default/files/94755_III.pdf

Hamilton, J. (2015, May). *1971: Citizens Who Exposed COINTELPRO.* PBS: Independent Lens. https://www.pbs.org/independentlens/documentaries/1971/

Hoover, J. Edgar. (n.d.). *"The FBI Sets Goals for COINTELPRO,"* SHEC: Resources for Teachers. City University of New York. https://shec.ashp.cuny.edu/items/show/814

Introduction and Summary. Intelligence Activities and the Rights of Americans—Church Committee final report. II. (1976, April). United States Senate. p. 10.

Jalon, Allan M. (2006, March 8). *A break-in to end all break-ins.* Los Angeles Times. https://web.archive.org/web/20131203035850/http:/articles.latimes.com/2006/mar/08/opinion/oe-jalon8

Johnson, M. (2002, January). *The Dangers of Domestic Spying by Federal Law Enforcement.* American Civil Liberties Union. https://web.archive.org/web/20180205173958/https:/www.aclu.org/files/FilesPDFs/mlkreport.pdf

Kane, G. (2000, May 14). *FBI should acknowledge complicity in the assassination of Malcolm X.* Baltimore Sun. https://www.baltimoresun.com/news/bs-xpm-2000-05-14-0005140182-story.html

Lewis, D. (2005). Guide to the Microfilm Edition of FBI Surveillance Files: FBI Files On Black Extremist Organizations, Part 1. *Lexis-Nexis.* ISBN 0-88692-739-0. https://web.archive.org/web/20130603094342/http:/cisupa.proquest.com/ksc_assets/catalog/101095_FBIBlackExtrOrgsPt1COINTELPRO.pdf

Murder of Fred Hampton. (2010, February). It's About Time—Black Panther Party Legacy & Alumni. http://www.itsabouttimebpp.com/home/home.html

Rowan, Carl T. *(1991). Breaking Barriers: A Memoir (1st ed.).* Little Brown & Co. p. 260. ISBN 978-0316759779.

Swearingen, M.W. (1995). *FBI Secrets: An Agent's Expose.* South End Press. ISBN 978-0896085022.

Walby, K., & Monaghan, J. (2011). Private Eyes and Public Order: Policing and Surveillance in the Suppression of Animal Rights Activists in Canada. *Social Movement Studies, 10*(1), 21–37. https://doi.org/10.1080/14742837.2011.545225

Weiner, T. (2012). *Enemies: A History of the FBI* (1st ed.). New York: Random House. pp. 198, 235-236. ISBN: 978-1400067480.

Wolf, P. (2001, September). *COINTELPRO: The Untold American Story.* World Conference Against Racism. Durbin, South Africa. Archive.org. p. 11.

#35 Voting Rights Act (1965)

About Section 5 of the Voting Rights Act. (n.d.). *U.S. Department of Justice.* https://www.justice.gov/crt/about-section-5-voting-rights-act

African Americans—The Civil War era. (n.d.). Encyclopedia Britannica. https://www.britannica.com/topic/African-American/The-Civil-War-era

History of Federal Voting Rights Laws: The Voting Rights Act of 1965. Civil Rights Division. (2015, August). *United States Department of Justice.* https://www.justice.gov/crt/history-federal-voting-rights-laws

History of Federal Voting Rights Laws: The Voting Rights Act of 1965. (2017, July). *United States Department of Justice.* https://archive.md/rTJ7q

History.com Editors. (2021, November 30). *Voting Rights Act of 1965.* HISTORY. https://www.history.com/topics/black-history/voting-rights-act

Introduction to Federal Voting Rights Laws: The Effect of the Voting Rights Act. (2009, June). *United States Department of Justice.* https://www.justice.gov/crt/introduction-federal-voting-rights-laws-0

Lewis, J., & Allen, A.E. (1972, October 1). *Black Voter Registration Efforts in the South*. Notre Dame. https://scholarship.law.nd.edu/cgi/viewcontent. cgi?article=2861&context=ndlr

Pilgrim, D. (2012). *What was Jim Crow*. Ferris State University-Jim Crow Museum of Racist Memorabilia. https://www.ferris.edu/jimcrow/what.htm

Racial and Ethnic Tensions in American Communities: Poverty, Inequality, and Discrimination Volume VII: The Mississippi Delta Report, Chapter 3 Voting Rights and Political Representation in the Mississippi Delta (n.d.). *United States Commission on Civil Rights*. https://www.usccr.gov/files/pubs/msdelta/ch3.htm

South Carolina v. Katzenbach, 383 US 301. (1966). *United States Supreme Court.*

Voting Rights Act (1965): Document Info. Our Documents. *United States National Archives and Records Administration.* https://www.ourdocuments.gov/doc. php?flash=true&doc=100

Voting Rights Act. (n.d.). National Voting Rights Museum and Institute. http://nvrmi.com/?page_id=41

Voting Rights Act: Major Dates in History. (n.d.). American Civil Liberties Union. https://www.aclu.org/voting-rights-act-major-dates-history

White, I.K. & Laird, C.N. (2020, February 25). *Why are Blacks Democrats?* Princeton. https://press.princeton.edu/ideas/why-are-blacks-democrats

#36 Modern Day (1968–Present)

A Changing America: 1968 and BEYOND (n.d.). National Museum of African American History & Culture. https://nmaahc.si.edu/changing-america

African Americans—The Civil War era. (n.d.). Encyclopedia Britannica. https://www.britannica.com/topic/African-American/The-Civil-War-era

An overview of the African American experience. (n.d.). Constitutional Rights Foundation. https://www.crf-usa.org/Black-history-month/ an-overview-of-the-african-american-experience

Solomon D., Maxwell, C., & Castro, A. (2019, August). *Systemic Inequality and American Democracy*. Center for American Progress. https://www.americanprogress.org/issues/ race/reports/2019/08/07/473003/systematic-inequality-american-democracy/

#37 Modern Day Era Voter Suppression Tactics

A Changing America: 1968 and BEYOND. (n.d.). National Museum of African American History & Culture. https://nmaahc.si.edu/changing-america

African American Senators. (n.d.). United States Senate. https://www.senate.gov/history/ Photo_Exhibit_African_American_Senators.htm

An overview of the African American experience. (n.d.). Constitutional Rights Foundation. https://www.crf-usa.org/Black-history-month/ an-overview-of-the-african-american-experience

Britannica, T. Editors of Encyclopedia (2021, May 6). *Pinckney Benton Stewart Pinchback*. Encyclopedia Britannica. https://www.britannica.com/biography/Pinckney-Benton-Stewart-Pinchback

Harper, A. (2021, January 19). *Capitol attack conjures American legacy of racial violence*. ABC News. https://abcnews.go.com/Politics/capitol-attack-conjures-american-legacy-racial-violence/story?id=75331177

Lynch, H. (2021, September 9). *African Americans*. Encyclopedia Britannica. https://www.britannica.com/topic/African-American

Morrison, A., Stafford, K., & Fernando, C. (2020, November 22). *Trump election challenges sound alarm among voters of color*. The Associated Press. https://apnews.com/article/joe-biden-donald-trump-race-and-ethnicity-georgia-wisconsin-a2f5155019a0c5aa09a7a6a82fb7d14b

Solomon D., Maxwell, C., & Castro, A. (2019, August). *Systemic Inequality and American Democracy*. Center for American Progress. https://www.americanprogress.org/issues/race/reports/2019/08/07/473003/systematic-inequality-american-democracy/

Stafford, K., Morrison, A., & Kastanis, A., (2020, November 9). *'This is proof': Biden's win reveals power of Black voters*. The Associated Press. https://apnews.com/article/election-2020-joe-biden-race-and-ethnicity-virus-outbreak-georgia-7a843bbce00713cfde6c3fdbc2e31eb7

Winkleman, A., & Debinski, G. (2021, January). *The Graphic Truth: Black representation in the US Congress*. GZERO Media. https://www.gzeromedia.com/the-graphic-truth-black-representation-in-the-us-congress

#38 Affirmative Action

A Brief History of Affirmative Action. (n.d.). University of California, Irvine, Office of Equal Opportunity and Diversity. http://www.oeod.uci.edu/policies/aa_history.php

Affirmative Action. (n.d.). Cornell Law School. https://www.law.cornell.edu/wex/affirmative_action#:~:text=While%20the%20concept%20of%20affirmative,are%20treated%20during%20employment%2C%20without

Affirmative Action. (n.d.). Oxford Dictionaries. Oxford University Press. https://www.lexico.com/definition/affirmative_action

Affirmative Action. (2018, April 9). Stanford Encyclopedia of Philosophy. https://plato.stanford.edu/entries/affirmative-action/

African Americans—A new direction. (n.d.). Encyclopedia Britannica. https://www.britannica.com/topic/African-American/A-new-direction

Bakke v. Regents of the University of California, 18 Cal. 3d 34, 132 Cal. Rptr. 680, 553 P.2d 1152. (1976, September 16). Supreme Court of California. https://scholar.google.com/scholar_case?case=5269915948665529282

Britannica, T. Editors of Encyclopedia (2021, June 21). *Bakke decision*. Encyclopedia Britannica. https://www.britannica.com/event/Bakke-decision

Cose, E. 1998. *Color-Blind: Seeing Beyond Race in a Race-Obsessed World*. Harper Perennial. ISBN 978-0060928872.

Cozzi, N. (2018, August 16). *White Women and Affirmative Action*. The Commission for Social Justice Education Blog. https://acpacsje.wordpress.com/2018/08/16/White-women-and-affirmative-action-by-nicole-cozzi/

Dreyfuss, Joel (1979). *The Bakke Case: The Politics of Inequality* (1st Ed.). Harcourt Brace Jovanovich. ISBN 978-0156167826.

Executive Order 10925-Establishing the President's Committee on Equal Employment Opportunity. (n.d.). United States Department of Labor. https://www.presidency.ucsb.edu/documents/executive-order-10925-establishing-the-presidents-committee-equal-employment-opportunity

Executive Order 11246—Equal Employment Opportunity. (n.d.) United States Department of Labor. https://www.dol.gov/agencies/ofccp/executive-order-11246/ca-11246

Executive Order 11246—Equal employment opportunity. (2016, August 15). The Federal Register. https://www.archives.gov/federal-register/codification/executive-order/11246.html

Freedburg, L. (1998, June 27). *After 20 Years, Bakke Ruling Back in the Spotlight / Foes of college affirmative action want high court to overturn it*. SF Gate. https://www.sfgate.com/politics/article/After-20-Years-Bakke-Ruling-Back-in-the-3003000.php

Hall, P. D. (2016). White Fragility and Affirmative Action. *The Journal of Race & Policy*, 12(2), pp 7-21.

History.com Editors. (2021, April 27). Black History Milestones: Timeline. HISTORY. https://www.history.com/topics/black-history/black-history-milestones

Kohn, S. (2013, June) *Affirmative Action Has Helped White Women More Than Anyone*. Time. https://time.com/4884132/affirmative-action-civil-rights-white-women/

MacLaury, J. (2010) *President Kennedy's E.O.10925: Seedbed of Affirmative Action*. Federal History. http://www.shfg.org/resources/Documents/FH%202%20(2010)%20MacLaury.pdf

Massie, V. M. (2016, June 23). *White women benefit most from affirmative action—and are among its fiercest opponents*. Vox. https://www.vox.com/2016/5/25/11682950/fisher-supreme-court-white-women-affirmative-action

Positive Discrimination. (n.d.). Oxford Dictionaries. Oxford University Press. https://www.lexico.com/en/definition/positive_discrimination

'The Job of Ending Discrimination in This Country Is Not Over'—Full text of President Clinton's July 19, 1995, speech on affirmative action. (1995, July 19). Washington Post. https://www.washingtonpost.com/wp-srv/politics/special/affirm/docs/clintonspeech.htm

Wise, T. (1998, September 23). *Is Sisterhood Conditional?: White Women and the Rollback of Affirmative Action*. National Women's Studies Association Journal. http://www.timwise.org/1998/09/is-sisterhood-conditional-white-women-and-the-rollback-of-affirmative-action/

#39 Crack Epidemic (1980s–1990s)

Abadinsky, H. (2013). *Drug Use and Abuse: A Comprehensive Introduction.* Cengage Learning. ISBN 978-1305161641.

DEA History Book, 1985–1990. (1991). United States Department of Justice/ Drug Enforcement Administration. https://www.dea.gov/sites/default/files/2021-04/1985-1990_p_58-67.pdf

Dockterman, E. (2014, October). *This Is the Real Story Behind Kill the Messenger.* Time. https://time.com/3482909/this-is-the-real-story-behind-kill-the-messenger/

Durbin's Fair Sentencing Act Passed by House, Sent to President for Signature. (2010, July 28). durbin.senate.gov. https://www.durbin.senate.gov/newsroom/press-releases/durbins-fair-sentencing-act-passed-by-house-sent-to-president-for-signature

Leen, J. (2014, October 17). *Gary Webb was no journalism hero, despite what 'Kill the Messenger' says.* The Washington Post. https://www.washingtonpost.com/opinions/gary-webb-was-no-journalism-hero-despite-what-kill-the-messenger-says/2014/10/17/026b7560-53c9-11e4-809b-8cc0a295c773_story.html

National Research Council. (2014). *The Growth of Incarceration in the United States: Exploring Causes and Consequences.* The National Academies Press. ISBN 978-0309298018. https://www.nap.edu/read/18613/chapter/4

Opioid Overdose Deaths by Race/Ethnicity (2001-2018). (n.d.) Kaiser Family Foundation. https://www.kff.org/other/state-indicator/opioid-overdose-deaths-by-raceethnicity/?activeTab=graph&currentTimeframe=1&startTimeframe=18&sortModel=%7B%22colId%22:%22Location%22,%22sort%22:%22asc%22%7D

Ray, R. & Galston, W. (2020, August 28). *Did the 1994 crime bill cause mass incarceration?.* The Brookings Institution. https://www.brookings.edu/blog/fixgov/2020/08/28/did-the-1994-crime-bill-cause-mass-incarceration/

The CIA-CONTRA-Crack Cocaine Controversy: A Review of the Justice Department's Investigations and Prosecutions. (1997, December). United States Department of Justice/Office Inspector General Special Report. https://oig.justice.gov/sites/default/files/archive/special/9712/index.htm

The War on Drugs. (n.d.). Crime Museum. https://www.crimemuseum.org/crime-library/drugs/the-war-on-drugs/

Turner, D. S. (2017, September 4). *crack epidemic.* Encyclopedia Britannica. https://www.britannica.com/topic/crack-epidemic

2015 Report to the Congress: Impact of the Fair Sentencing Act of 2010. (2015, August). United States Sentencing Commission. https://www.ussc.gov/sites/default/files/pdf/news/congressional-testimony-and-reports/drug-topics/201507_RtC_Fair-Sentencing-Act.pdf

#40 De Facto Segregation

African American Senators. (n.d.). United States Senate. https://www.senate.gov/history/ Photo_Exhibit_African_American_Senators.htm

America's Opportunity Gaps: By the Numbers. (2020, June). U.S. Chamber of Commerce. https://www.uschamber.com/workforce/education/us-chamber-releases-america-s-opportunity-gaps-the-numbers-examining-underlying

Britannica, T. Editors of Encyclopedia (2021, May 6). *Pinckney Benton Stewart Pinchback*. Encyclopedia Britannica. https://www.britannica.com/biography/ Pinckney-Benton-Stewart-Pinchback

de facto. (n.d.). The Merriam-Webster.Com Dictionary. https://www.merriam-webster.com/ dictionary/de%20facto

Longley, R. (2021, February 21). *What is De Facto Segregation? Definition and Current Examples*. ThoughtCo. https://www.thoughtco.com/ de-facto-segregation-definition-4692596#

Smietana. B. (2015, January 15). *Sunday Morning in America Still Segregated— and That's OK with Worshipers*. Lifeway Research. https://lifewayresearch.com/2015/01/15/sunday-morning-in-america-still-segregated-and-thats-ok-with-worshipers/

Winkleman, A., & Debinski, G. (2021, January). *The Graphic Truth: Black representation in the US Congress*. GZERO Media. https://www.gzeromedia.com/ the-graphic-truth-black-representation-in-the-us-congress

INDEX